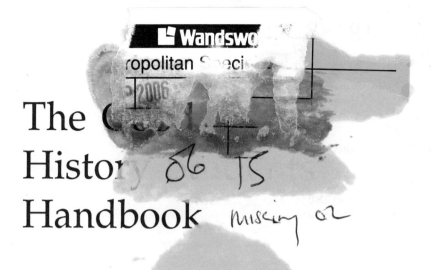

The Cold War
History δ6 TS
Handbook muscing oz

Edited by Gilbert Pleuger

Sempringham *publis*

First published in 1993
by Sempringham publishing
11 St Augustine's Road
Bedford MK40 2NB
Bedford (0234) 267856

© History Review 1993
History Review
20 Old Compton Street
London W1V 5PE

ISBN 0 9515764 1 0

Cover drawing by Stephen Odom
Designed and typeset by Sempringham publishing
Printed and bound by Arca Press, Bedford MK42 0EU

CONTENTS

Core Concepts, Terms and Ideologies

The Student and Evidence

Acknowledgements

This volume is assembled from specially commissioned chapters
and from study skills articles which were first published in
History Review (or, *History Sixth*, retitled in September 1991).
The Editor acknowledges, with gratitude, the consent of the
contributors to the inclusion of their articles and, for permission
to reprint the articles, to Gordon Marsden, Editor of *History Today*
- the publication to whom the copyright passed in 1992.

It is opportune to thank, in addition, all the contributors to the
journal since its foundation in 1987. Without articles of admirable
quality which the authors readily contributed to *History Review*
this journal, which grew out of the department magazine at
Bedford School, would not have served generations of Advanced
Level and younger undergraduates as a complement to texts and
monographs and as an encouragement to debate and
to reconsider well-worked topics.

Exclusive to the above paragraphs, permission to reprint articles
is acknowledged from Little Brown for chapter 2, 'Making Notes',
which was originally published in *Learn How to Study*, first edition
1970, and to Guardian Newspapers Ltd for chapter 8, 'How to
Manage with Time', which was first published on 24 September
1991 in *The Guardian* under the title 'Schedule for passing the test
of time'.

Why History Matters

THE VARIOUS ARGUMENTS currently put forward against the study of history really follow one of two lines. One complains of what has become known as elitism: why should the generality involve itself with long-gone persons of supposed eminence - with kings and nobles and their likes? It is all a waste of time and especially an unnecessary burdening of the memory. The other argument is more positive. It maintains that the present should free itself of the burden of history; it should look to its own concerns and to the future. A preoccupation with the past is reckoned to be intellectually wrong and morally misleading; besides, all those memories, accurate or not, merely prevent sensible action in solving the problems of the present day. Let the dead past bury its dead, and so forth. These doubts have of late been reinforced by some lavish theories derived from language studies: deconstruction and post-modernism (deep mysteries resolved to deny the existence of the human reason) have convinced too many people that there is no such thing as historical truth. Everything said is supposedly merely a construct put forward by the so-called historians who treat the evidence of the past as a 'text' that they can read any way they please while pretending to relate what that past meant by it. Now it is true that we can never arrive at a totally truthful and unchallengeable understanding of past events: we work on evidence that is both incomplete and ambiguous, and interpretation therefore comes into the exercise. But perfectly valid and effective principles to control the historian's duty to interpret have been worked out: we all talk to one another about our common concerns under rules and by insights that severely limit our personal interventions. Preconceived notions and prejudices exist but are quite easily kept within necessary restraints - far more easily than all those philosophers who have never worked on history would seem to suppose. Historical knowledge cannot be perfect, and historical understanding develops by means of argument and sometimes of controversy, but what emerges - though it may change and develop - is a good deal more assured, and contains far more aspects of reality and establishable truth, than the fancies of self-satisfied speculators would profess. That is to say, history is a true subject of study and worth pursuing for that reason alone, though other benefits exist and shall be listed. Moreover, the intellectual methods of the historian set a very useful example to the student at every stage: though only a minority will come to practise history, just about everybody can gain advantages from following the practitioners' path.

Indeed, the hope that the present might 'free itself' from the alleged burden of history is altogether vain as well as rather silly. As each moment passes it becomes history: we all live in and by history. Which fact surely is as good a reason as any for learning about the past, not in order to dictate to the present but in order to provide a three-dimensional view of the human existence. Since we cannot escape from history we should concentrate on the benefits that a study of it can bring.

History and Human Behaviour

We might start from the fact that much of history - the learned study of the past - is very interesting and often exciting. It is by no means as dry as it often appears to the student who has been led to believe that he is supposed to memorise lists, tables and dates. History is about human behaviour and all that that involves: human behaviour, human ambitions and human relations can be positively amusing as well as highly instructive. All that is here required is a touch of imagination, a serious effort to penetrate past mere laboured seriousness and reasonable accuracy to a close relationship to the people studied. By this I do not mean what is usually called empathy: empathy, a form of condescension, puts the student rather than the object studied at the centre of the operation. It asks us to bestow our kindly sympathy on the people of the past, rather than allow ourselves to seek the benefits which the people of the past stand ready to bestow upon us. Empathetic endeavours will reduce those people to agents for the investigator's own notions, foibles and ambitions. If we are to obtain the real profits offered by historical study we must reduce ourselves to at best a very subordinate position in the enterprise and open ourselves to the thoughts and deeds of people no longer with us, people and thoughts and deeds in their own right, understood from within their own world and conditions. This is not an easy thing to do, but difficulties exist to be overcome, not to be surrendered to. History accords primacy to the subject studied and endeavours to reduce to a minimum the agency through which the experience passes in the present.

Properly handled, the treatment of the past for its own sake chalks up one manifest gain and disallows one frequently advanced but in fact illusory use of historical study. The gain consists in the enormous enlargement of one's acquaintance. Involving oneself in the past means to meet shoals of people - people often very different in standing, mind and achievement from those we encounter within the necessarily limited range of our living experience. Far more men and women, and men and women doing and feeling very unfamiliar things: the honest historian learns to know so many human beings, some of them interesting in themselves and others less so, that he acquires a well based and well ordered understanding of humanity. One of the first things to strike the mind that approaches this task without undue preconceptions can be disconcerting; it soon becomes clear that people do not by any means always behave as theories about behaviour or interest prescribe. (This is why Marxist history has gone so sadly astray, but so did the predestinarian Christian history of an earlier age.) Unpredictability and free will come to dominate the scene. History shows that you can explain what happened and why, but that you cannot really foretell the outcome until it has happened.

From this somewhat uncomfortable realisation there follows the sad conclusion that what is commonly put forward as the most important product of historical knowledge does not really work. History is not automatically a good guide for action in the present and the future: knowing and comprehending the past does not efficiently equip one for foretelling what will happen. Historians are not prophets, a fact that they should accept. The recent collapse of communist regimes in Eastern Europe provides an excellent example: first, events totally surprised (and silenced) pro-communist historians, and within a few months developments appeared which totally contradicted (though they did not silence) those historians who had welcomed the event. However, this in no way demolishes the usefulness of historical knowledge - the wide acquaintance with people and events of all sorts - that the sensible student acquires. The historian comes to understand situations and the people moving within them: what he gains is human understanding though not instructions as to action. He should, of course, pay heed to the various forms of study that mankind has worked out for its fate and fortunes - to economics, sociology, anthropology, literature and the arts, and so forth. Everything humanly done or thought of is his province, provided it lies before his own time. His understanding how things happened in that past time also equips him with the right and power to criticise general theories or lesser comprehensive schemata that those other forms of investigation tend to throw up: in the face of assertions which lack real proof or can be historically disproven, he manifests a carefully modulated scepticism. This critical power constitutes an important social role for which no other study offers anything like so effective a training.

The Historical Method

Fulfilling that role does, however, call for some hard work and clear thinking. Several of the essays in this volume bear on this point, but it may be useful here to distil the essence of the historical method which justifies a sceptical approach to other people's views. Every problem involves three main stages of research: a review of the available evidence, the informed criticism of that evidence (what exactly does it testify to?), and the framing of answers to the questions posed. That is the right sequence: to reverse it by following the often heard advice that questions should be precisely framed before the evidence has been reviewed with their help nearly always produces answers arrived at before the investigation. The good historian does not narrow down his enquiry until he has become reasonably well acquainted with the past speaking through what it left behind. For example, one may wish to find out why there was a civil war in seventeenth-century England. The fact of that war can be accepted but what are usually called its causes should be the end of the enquiry, not the beginning. Thus it would be wrong to start by assuming that the split within the nation represented a fundamental division along, for instance, lines of religious beliefs and then to search for evidence to substantiate this. One must first cover the range of evidence for attitudes, beliefs and actions with a mind alert to all possibilities. Such a first investigation will itself put up specific questions, but they will arise from the evidence not from the mind of the enquirer. At this stage, the historian, so far the servant of his evidential material, takes charge and seeks specific answers. In this way he avoids a risk to which much historical writing has before this fallen victim: the risk that it is he and not the past that decides what happened.

The second stage of the operation - the critical assessment of the available evidence - will then be governed by the double awareness of the general scene in which the evidence was produced and the particular issues which it brings into the open. Since this involves the historian's positive intervention he must be particularly careful to avoid injecting preconceived notions, for instance about the relative scale of possible motives: he should still allow the materials he uses to tell their story, so far as he possibly can. On the other hand, the third stage of the operation releases everything to him. Having made himself master as well as servant of both the material and the questions, he can get down to framing his reconstruction, reasonably confident that he is not merely justifying a preconceived point of view but is getting as near the truth of the past as he has any hope of getting. For historians have to come to terms with the inevitable incompleteness of their labours. Since all that the past has left behind is haphazard, patchy and often uncertain evidence, the historian's judgement, however well trained in the principles of right scholarship, will in the end have to choose between possibilities rather than present unquestionably precise conclusions. Hence also those frequent debates among historians which to some people outside the game look like mere wars of self-importance. Historical knowledge most commonly advances in the crucible of debate, a crucible which tends to preserve

something of every seriously advanced point of view and by
stages creates better knowledge. That is why what some people
call revisionism appears at present to be so rampant among
historians. Entrenched interpretations in due course call forth
legitimate doubt and questioning; in the process evidence both old
and new is more thoroughly scrutinised; new and usually better
based conclusions emerge. Human nature being what it is, the
debaters too often become combatants and differences of opinion
are made to look like rival faiths, but that superficial appearance
misleads. At issue is the truth of history not the person of the
historian, and few debaters forget this fact. One may hope that
the language of debate will retain reasonable courtesies and
respect the adversary. All attempts to recover the truth of history
are bound to be sufficiently incomplete to permit A to think B
mistaken but not corrupt.

Thus the study of history matters because it produces better
experienced human beings, who are more balanced and humane.
Furthermore, a grasp of history and its methods enables reason to
subject overconfident and often menacing policy positions to
informed criticism. The main profit lies in the unending interest of
historical studies. Because they never arrive at a final end and
indisputable answer to every question posed they also never
cease. Most scholarly labours, once framed as problems, come to
an end, and many workers in the realms of the mind find their
enterprise concluding before their lives do. Historians go on to the
end of their days, living in and with the past, finding new
problems and issues to pursue, revising old problems and issues
to new conclusions. In short, doing history is endlessly exciting
and a lovely way to spend one's days.

Sir Geoffrey Elton. Clare College, Cambridge.

The
History Student's
Study Skills

1

Reading for History Students

HISTORY TEXTBOOKS tend to be fat, wouldn't you agree? Fortunately, authors and publishers are increasingly aware of how off-putting pages of close set type can be and do their best to break it up with summaries of key dates, questions to think about, maps, and extracts from historical documents. But there's no getting away from it - the evil moment comes every week, when there is no alternative but to get down to your reading.

If you find your eyelids grow heavy, and you turn the page without a clue about what you've just read, then this article is for you. Read on.

Don't settle down to read every word though. How much time have you got to devote to this article? You don't at this point know if what I'm going to say is of any relevance or interest to you, and your time is precious. So how do you know in advance of reading a piece whether it's worth taking time over or not?

Try the common-sense approach to reading you use in everyday life. Think about how you read notices on a crowded noticeboard, for example. If you are looking for a particular item for sale, you will *scan* the whole board, barely registering the majority of the notices as you search for a single item. A few you will *skim* read briefly - long enough to register that the item isn't what you want, and then you speed on. You will probably only *read in detail* one or two notices, the ones you want to think about. You may *re-read* these to make sure you have all the details, and to *make notes* - in this case, details of the item, contact phone number and address. One thing is certain; you do not read systematically through every single notice, starting at the top left hand corner down to the bottom right, making copious notes of the entire contents of the For Sale board!

How then do you apply this common-sense efficiency in reading to the sorts of reading you have to do in your studies? Take a closer look at the processes you would have used on the noticeboard:

- SURVEY your reading matter critically - title/chapter heading, subtitle, author, date of publication, contents, index. Do the chapters have summaries or lists of key points or dates at the beginning or end? If so, read this *first*. The survey should take a minute or two. It is a vital first stage. Don't skip it.

- QUESTION yourself about what exactly you are expecting to get out of the book or chapter, to keep your reading active and your concentration good.

- READ! Reading is the third, not the first and last stage in active reading. By now you can pinpoint what you are going to read and what you want to get out of your reading. But don't settle down to read every word. As with the notice-board, you will *skim* some bits for an overview; *scan* others for a particular piece of information; *read in detail* only those sections you absolutely have to. I hope to convince you in the reading exercises which follow (pp. 11-13), that relatively little needs to be read in detail, and that you can get the main points out of most paragraphs by skilful skim reading.

- RECALL What have you just read? Can you answer the questions you set yourself at the outset? Now is the time to make your notes. But don't copy. Set out the main points as you remember them. Leave lots of space to add detail and check with the text if you need to.

- REVIEW Quickly look back over the text to make sure you haven't missed anything or distorted points in your notes. Skim read.

This strategic approach to reading - Survey, Question, Read, Recall, Review or SQ3R for short - will save you time and effort. You may enjoy the challenge of tackling a jigsaw without looking at the picture, but of course it is easier when you know roughly where the pieces fit. The same with reading - the detail makes sense more quickly when you have an overview.

Of the three reading techniques I've mentioned, skimming is probably the most underused. If you are to skim read effectively, you need to know where to look for the main idea in a paragraph since paragraphs are the units that make up longer sections. To do this, you need to think about how writing is structured.

In your own writing, when you move on to a new idea, you start a new paragraph. Your plan for an answer to the essay question, 'Have the achievements of the Elizabethan seamen been exaggerated?' will have points for and points against. Each of these points will be developed into paragraphs in your essay. You start each paragraph with your point expressed as clearly as possible. The sentence in which the writer expresses this new or main idea is known as the 'topic sentence'.

The topic sentence is usually the first sentence in the paragraph. In the middle of the paragraph the writer explains, develops and illustrates this idea. The last sentence often directly picks up the idea in the topic sentence and shows how the rest of the paragraph has modified or developed it.

- *Try it. Look back at the last two paragraphs. Do they follow this pattern? For each, pick out*

  i   the beginning: topic sentence

  ii   the middle: explanation, illustration

  iii the end; linking back to the idea in the topic sentence.

They do, don't they? So it stands to reason that if you want to know what a paragraph is about, you read the first sentence. If you want to see how a writer has developed the idea, read the last sentence as well.

- *Read only the first sentence of the first four paragraphs of this article.*

How much would you have missed if you had only read these sentences and not the whole paragraph? Not a lot I reckon. The first paragraph was a general introduction to the sorts of reading you have to do in history, and offers, I hope, some encouragement to read on. The second has no development and cannot really be termed a paragraph. A short paragraph like this every now and again breaks up the reading task, but too many short paragraphs suggests that the writer does not know how to develop an idea, and is simply listing points - a bad sign at A Level. 'Don't settle down to read every word . . .' in the third paragraph gives a clear indication of what that paragraph is about as does the first sentence in the fourth paragraph.

- *Now read the first and last sentences of the third and fourth paragraphs.*

In these two paragraphs, the last sentence links clearly back to the first.

Skim reading the topic sentence of a paragraph should give you a clear indication of what the paragraph is about. If you then decide to read the paragraph, it's because you think the paragraph has something to offer you. Your *survey* and *questioning* have pinpointed something for *detailed* reading.

- *Does any of the first four paragraphs look worth a closer look?*

My guess is paragraph four, if any. Here the article begins to get down to the nitty gritty of reading strategies. Alternatively, you may have surveyed the rest of the article, realised that this paragraph too was introductory and have decided to plunge in perhaps round about here. Good for you!

- *Read only the first sentence of each paragraph in the following extract, once only, and answer the following questions.*

  i)   What is known about a) pupil numbers and b) the quality of education in the mid-nineteenth century?

  ii) What was the response of the authorities to this?

Educational statistics show a steady rise in pupil numbers but the overall quality of education is unmeasurable. It is known that absenteeism was common and that education was frequently regarded as a subordinate function of childhood. As late as 1840, probably one-third of all children never attended a day school. Since the length of education for working class children rarely exceeded three and a half years, and was commonly less than two, levels of attainment even from reputable establishments cannot have been high.

The lack of control over educational output caused increasing alarm. In the early 1830s, roughly 60 per cent of all schools were private, rather than church, establishments and many feared, as had Davies Giddy MP in 1807, that in these ordinary folk would learn to read 'seditious pamphlets, vicious books and publications against Christianity' (260,9). Church schools, by contrast, were regarded as safe.

(The Forging of the Modern State 1783-1870 by Eric J. Evans, Longman, 1983, p. 232.)

• *Now skim read the extract, first and last sentences only, and see what additional information you gain.*

Did you need to read the whole paragraph to have a pretty good idea of what it is about? There may be times when you do need figures and names, but if you do, you know where to find them, You don't need this information for routine background reading.

• *Try skim reading again, this time on a longer extract. Read only the first sentence of each paragraph. The question in your mind before you start reading is 'What is this paragraph going to be about?' Jot down your expectation of what each paragraph will be about after you have read the topic sentence.*

Not only was Charles a threat to Francis but also the reverse was true. Charles had the difficulty of co-ordinating men and money from scattered territories, with France eager to exploit any weakness in the chain. Meanwhile, France as a unitary state did not experience the same logistical problems and could strike at whichever part of the empire seemed vulnerable. Charles was a man of integrity and he found the unscrupulous Francis very hard to deal with, especially when the latter allied with the great enemy of Christendom, the Ottoman Empire.

There were also other irritants to drive the two sides apart. Italy had been a battleground since the fifteenth century and only domination by one side would end the conflict there. Charles wished to regain Burgundy, the ancestral home of his dynasty, annexed by France in 1477. Similarly the incorporation of Navarre into Castile was not recognised by France. These old disputes could be revived whenever circumstances seemed appropriate (so France could take advantage of the revolt of the *Comuneros* by reasserting claims to Navarre).

Ultimately, Francis I could not tolerate Charles' claim to dominance. The latter might protest, as he did in 1536. 'There are those who say that I wish to rule the world, but both my thoughts and my deeds demonstrate the contrary'. But this was hardly enough to dissuade Francis from plotting the downfall of his great rival.

The effect upon Charles' policies was immediately apparent. Decisive action against the emergent German Protestantism had to be postponed and, not for the last time, the internal needs of Charles' empire were sacrificed to the struggle against 'the most Christian' King of France.

(*Years of Renewal. European History 1470-1600* ed John Lotherington, Hodder and Stoughton 1988, p. 192.)

In this extract the topic sentences act as neon lights flashing up what is to follow. If you want to know more about the 'other irritants', driving Francis and Charles apart, for example, you can go back and read paragraph two in detail.

When you identify a piece you know you need to read in detail, do use the textual clues to make sure you have all the information. The phrase 'other irritants' suggests that not all the irritants are to follow - one at least has already been mentioned. Words like 'similarly' indicate that the point just made and the one about to be made are similar. Did you spot that? 'But' suggests a change of direction; 'meanwhile' points you to things happening simultaneously. Awareness of these 'markers' helps to keep your reading active, and you alert.

What I have proposed here is a strategy for reading. Don't adopt the donkey approach, munching through the pages. Take an active, critical approach to everything you have to read.

Make your reading matter: justify the time you spend on it.

>   *Survey* it first - is it relevant? Which bits? How long are the sections I have to read? Note the chapter and section headings. Look for the summary.

>   *Question* your purpose in reading. Be clear about what you expect to find out, and where it is likely to be.

Read in different ways according to your purpose. *Scan* for particular pieces of information. *Skim* for an overview of a section. *Read in detail* only when you have to, and only when you have located the information you need.

Recall what you've read, and make notes now.

Review the section, chapter or book for anything you've missed, and to help to 'fix' it in your mind.

• *A final reading activity. Scan this article to find the following:*

i   When was Burgundy annexed by France?

ii What proportion of children never attended school in the 1840s?

iii Where is the term 'marker' defined?

iv What is the date of publication of the book from which the first extract was taken?

v   What is the shorthand for the reading strategy I suggest?

vi Where do you normally find the topic sentence?

Aren't you glad you didn't have to read every word to extract this information from the article? You don't read every word of a newspaper, so why attempt it in your studies? It is not only slow, but inefficient. Vary your pace and style of reading according to your purpose at the time. This isn't cheating - it's intelligent reading.

Kate Williams is author of *Study Skills*, Macmillan, 1989.

2

Making Notes

MOST STUDENTS spend a lot of their time making notes. Why do they do it? What form do their notes take? What use do they make of them afterwards? Are they always worth the paper they are written on? These are the kinds of question that I will consider.

Why Make Notes?

As with all aspects of studying, the most appropriate way of making notes depends on your purpose. So, it is useful to be clear in your own mind about why you are making notes. Possible purposes:

1 'To help me understand what I'm hearing or reading about while I am studying it.'

2 'To ensure I keep paying attention.'

3 'To help me review the learning session afterwards.'

4 'To ensure I have as full a statement as possible of what was actually said.'

5 'To record my own thoughts or examples concerning what is being said.'

6 'To remind myself of follow-up reading, etc.'

7 'To have material to revise for exams.'

8 'To sort out my own ideas on a topic.'

9 'To plan my work for an assignment or in an exam.'

Looking at the list above, I see an important distinction between purposes 1-7 and 8-9. They distinguish between the kind of notes you might write when:

(a)   you are trying to respond to *someone else's ideas*
        e.g. from a lecture or a book

(b)   you are trying to produce and sort out *your own ideas*
        e.g. in planning an assignment.

Some people talk of (a) as 'taking notes' and (b) as 'making notes'. Unfortunately, this suggests that (a) is a passive process, rather like taking a recording. I believe it is more helpful to think of both as active, creative processes. For example, whatever notes you write about a book, you will be putting something of yourself into them. You can easily check how much of yourself you've put into your notes by seeing how differently a colleague will have written about the same book. You will have *made* something different of the book.

There are perhaps three main reasons for making notes:

1   To aid concentration.
2   To help understanding and/or creativity.
3   To have some kind of record for future use.

All of these are *potential* benefits. But you don't get them automatically. You have to keep the purpose in mind and let it shape the sort of notes you are writing. For example:

- Writing notes can keep you actively concentrating on what you are reading or hearing. *But,* in a lecture, you can become so concerned with noting what the lecturer has just said that you lose track of what she or he is saying now.

- Writing notes can aid your understanding - but only if you *think* about the meaning of what you are reading or hearing. If you are simply trying to get down a 'full statement', then you are probably restricting yourself to 'surface level learning'. You may know what was said, but not know what it meant.

- Writing notes can also provide a record for future use. But you need to know what sort of future use you have in mind - e.g. as a means of recalling the author's or lecturer's total argument, as a collection of choice examples to support an argument of your own, as guidance on further reading. Notes you wrote with one future use in mind might not be helpful for certain other future uses.

Many students report that they do not make as much use of their notes in the future as they expected to at the time they wrote them. They mention several reasons for this:

1 They can't find the notes they need among all the other notes they've written before and since.
2 They can't read their own writing.
3 They can read it but they don't know what it means.
4 Their ideas have developed so much since they wrote the notes they now seem trivial or half-baked.
5 Their notes are too sparse/too full/don't contain the kind of material they now need.

This list, which no doubt you can add to, touches on several problems we'll be looking at in the rest of this article.

So there are several different purposes you might have in writing notes. And there are several reasons why your note-making might not be as helpful to you as you had hoped.

When do You Make Notes?

There are far more opportunities for making worthwhile notes than some students realise. Many make notes only of what 'authority figures' (like lecturers and authors) have to say. It seems not to occur to them that their fellow-students or even non-students may make remarks (or stimulate thoughts of their own) that are worth making a note of.

The moral is to have a notebook and pencil within reach at all times. 'Never let a good idea escape unrecorded' whether it crops up in a seminar or conversation in a pub, or even when you're relaxing with your feet up in front of the television.

Three Ways of Writing Notes

There are many ways of writing notes. Which way you choose may vary with your purpose and your personal preference. You may be simply jotting down isolated points that happen to interest you. These might consist simply of a list of examples, brief quotations, references, sketches and so on. You may on the other hand, be aiming to make a record of an author's or lecturer's complete line of argument or framework of ideas. For this purpose, a more structured form of note-making seems necessary. There seem to be three basic approaches:

1 Straight prose summary.

2 Skeleton outline.

3 Patterned notes/spray diagram/spider chart.

These can no doubt be combined in several ways, and you may have developed quite different ways of your own.

Summary notes are a condensed version or precis of the original. They are usually written in continuous prose - more or less complete sentences and paragraphs. A *skeleton outline,* however, will make more use of single words and brief phrases and these will be set out as a list, using devices like headings and sub-headings, numbering, indentation, and so on.

The third form of notes goes by various names. Let's stick with *spray diagram* here. This also uses brief words and phrases but the layout is quite different. You start off by naming the topic of your notes in the centre of a page. Then you spray out lines from the centre, one for each major branch of the topic and each labelled with a few words. Each branch can then be subdivided further by spraying off yet more lines from it, each one again carrying the appropriate (brief) label. And so on, until the topic runs out of subdivisions. Connections between one subdivision and another can be shown with linking lines.

Each of these ways of writing notes is illustrated opposite. Look at the three sets of notes and consider:

(a) From which set of notes can you most easily spot the *main points* of the chapter?

(b) Which notes most clearly show up the *relationships* between ideas in the chapter?

(c) Can you see a use in of your study tasks for any of these forms of notes that you have *not* yet used?

What did you think were the strengths and weaknesses of these ways of noting the main points of a book? Many students say that summaries are easy to write but awkward to use again later on.

The Art of Reading Actively

Reading actively means reading questioningly & purposefully. Involves finding main ideas & important details & evaluating text

Main ideas will be found at all levels from book as a whole to individual paragraphs. May detect the more general main ideas at Survey stage of SQ3R – more specific ones at Read stage. Look especially for topic sentence in paragraph (often 1st or last)

Students often don't distinguish between main ideas & important details – esp if reading at surface level (can't see wood for trees)

Important details clarify or support main ideas (which are important to me?)

Look out for author's visual & verbal signposts (emphasis, special phrases, etc.) Don't overlook diagrams. Don't just skip difficulties – struggle on, re-read, discuss with other students/tutor

Evaluate the text. Be critical. Ask questions to probe author's facts, opinions, evidence, argument, bias etc. And what have I learned from it? If necessary, make notes & discuss with other students

Concentration is aided by seeking meaning (but see also Ch 4). Don't sacrifice understanding for speed but vary speed according to purpose in reading.

Summary notes.

The Art of Reading Actively

A Active = purposeful, critical, questioning
B Look for Main Ideas
  1 Survey (SQ3R) for general ones (Ch 5)
  2 Read paragraphs for more specific ones
    a) Each para usually has one main idea
    b) Usually in topic sentence (1st or last?)
C Look for Important Details
  1 e.g. proof, example, support for main idea
  2 Usually at least one per main idea
  3 Which do I consider important?
D In hunt for main idea and important details
  1 Watch for signposts
    a) Visual (layout, etc.)
    b) Verbal (clue words)
  2 Study diagrams, etc.
  3 Don't ignore difficulties
E Evaluate the text
  1 Be sceptical (Expect the author to prove)
  2 Compare with my own experience
  3 What do I get from it?
  4 Discuss with other students
F Make Notes
  1 If I need them (for my purposes)
  2 At Recall stage (of SQ3R)
  3 Compare with other students
G Concentrate
  1 By seeking understanding (not memorisation)
  2 and see Chapter 4 hints
H Vary reading speed
  1 according to purpose
  2 but not at expense of understanding

Skeleton outline.

They find that skeleton outlines are better at showing up both the main ideas and the relationships between them. What do you think?

Spray diagrams get a mixed reception. Some students go overboard for them, noticing how usefully they can reveal the way topics split up into sub-topics and so on, and how the visual pattern (a different 'picture' for each page of notes) can help fix them in your mind. They also comment on how

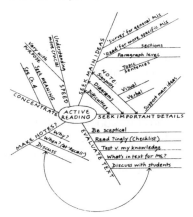

Spray diagram.

the lack of space forces you into using words and short phrases - thus making it less likely you will simply copy sentences from the author's text.

Other students complain that spray diagrams can't show the logical step-by-step structure of an argument. They also complain that they simply run out of space too quickly if they are trying to note material of any complexity - or else the page becomes too crowded and cramped to interpret later on. However, even some of those students admit that this may sometimes be a useful way of sorting out your own ideas as they occur to you, say, in planning an assignment. Some students write notes combining spray diagrams (to give an overview) with a summary to explain some of the details.

Notes in Different Circumstances

Notes from reading.

Here are some suggestions for making notes from books and articles.

1   Survey the book/article to check whether or not it is likely to contain anything worth noting.

2   Decide whether you will be making notes on the whole thing or merely sections of it.

3   Decide whether you want a complete outline of the author's argument or whether you are merely hoping to pick up a few bits of information (e.g. to add to what you already know).

4   Skim through each chosen chapter or section before you make notes so as to see the overall structure and identify some of the main ideas.

5   Read the material carefully, concentrating on what it means to you - not on what you are going to put in your notes.

6   Close the book, recall the main ideas and important details, draft some notes.

7   Review the section and amend your notes if you feel you've missed anything of significance, *but:*

• keep them *brief* - words and phrases rather than whole sentences (unless you need quotations)

• make sure you *use your own words* (unless you need quotations)

• distinguish in your notes between the author's ideas and ideas you have had while reading them.

The essence of effective note-making is selectivity. Many students seem to read with one finger tracing along the lines of their book while the other hand diligently copies down great chunks of the text. All they end up with is a mini-textbook. Thus twenty, thirty or more pages of text may boil down to a couple of pages of skeleton outline or spray diagrams. If you were merely looking for extra information to add to what you already know, then your notes from those thirty or so pages may amount to no more than a few lines (or nothing at all).

Making Notes in Lectures

That last piece of advice also applies to making notes in lectures. One definition of a lecture is 'A method for conveying the contents of the lecturer's notebook into that of the student without passing through the minds of either party'. Snide, but often true. Some lecturers do seem to content themselves with reading from their notes, or writing them on the board for you to copy. And some students seem satisfied to record as much as possible without pausing to ponder what it's all about.

Making useful notes in lectures depends on understanding what the lecturer means. This, in turn, depends on how you approach the lecture - surveying, questioning and listening. This listening is a very complex task. Not only must you pick out the lecturer's *main ideas* as he or she speaks, and grasp the overall *structure* of the lecture but also - and *at the same time* - you must decide what is worth noting and what is not.

This is no easy task. Some students deal with it by taking copious notes - often in summary form - and hoping to see some sort of pattern emerge from them after the lecture is over. Others concentrate on following the lecturer's line of argument, taking very few notes even if this means they don't record all the details.

On the whole, it is probably better to err on the side of too few notes rather than too many, provided:

1   This better enables you to concentrate on what the lecturer is saying and grasp the meaning and significance of what is said.

2   You are prepared to write up a full set of notes once the lecture is over.

That last point is essential, however full our lecture notes are. By comparison with reading notes they are likely to be scrappy and disorganised. Go away and rethink them.

Recalling a lecture. As soon as possible after the lecture, try to reconstruct it in your mind. Perhaps the most useful way to recall the lecture is in company with one or two other students - perhaps members of your self-help group. Comparing notes, you may find that different people have picked up different points and that, together, you can make a better set of notes - and better sense of what was said - than any one of you separately.

What Form of Notes?

Obviously, the form of notes you use will be much influenced by how clearly your lecturer indicates his or her structure. If the structure is clear, then you may be able to work up a reasonable skeleton outline - with headings, sub-headings, numbering, indentation and so on.

Otherwise, you may find it more practical to jot down points as they come, and sort them into a skeleton outline *after* the lecture.

You may also consider noting the lecture in the form of a spray diagram - so long as you don't let the mechanics involved distract you from thinking about what the lecturer is saying. And, again, you will probably need to tidy it up later on when you think back over the lecture.

Noting Your Own Ideas

As we mentioned earlier, not all your notes need arise in response to other people's ideas. Many students find the best way of sorting out their own ideas is to sit down with pencil and paper and jot down a few notes.

So, let's say you are sitting and thinking about a particular topic. It could be one you have studied, and you are simply trying to bring back to mind the main issues. It could be a new topic you are about to begin studying seriously and you are wondering what questions you already have about it. It could be a matter of how to tackle an assignment on a topic you are already familiar with.

In all these cases, and others like them, you don't have to go off in search of new information. All you need is in your head.

But how do you get it on to paper.

Most students jot down some sort of notes before starting to write an essay.

Brainstorming

One useful approach is 'brainstorming' - just muse upon the topic and jot down anything that comes to mind in connection with it. The essence of this approach is to write down everything just as it comes. Ideally, you shouldn't stop to decide whether some items look more useful than others or in what order they might be dealt with. Only when you have run out of ideas, and perhaps have a lengthy list, should you start to consider which look most promising, and how they might be developed and structured into a logical sequence. Thus, before I began writing this chapter, I jotted down a list of items beginning:

- Why make notes?
- How used?
- Are they used?
- What forms?
- When written?

An Ideas Map

I then found it helpful to rough out a diagram trying to link up the main ideas I picked out from my list. As you see, it looks rather like a spray diagram, but is much looser. (We might call it an 'ideas map'.) I've simply jotted down my ideas and drawn lines between those I think have some sort of connection. It looks a bit of a mess, but it served a purpose. It helped me decide how to structure the

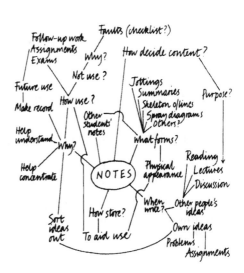

chapter and from it I produced a skeleton outline to guide my first draft.

Sometimes I find it helpful to sketch out an ideas map as part of my initial brainstorm rather than after I've finished it. Roughing out such an 'ideas map' may strike you as a useful way of sorting through your ideas on a topic - regardless of whether you have first done a brainstorm. As always, it is up to you to experiment with a variety of approaches and find out what suits you best. In writing an essay, for example, some students might be quite confident about launching in with an ideas map (or even just a list of points) while others (and I'd be one of them) would not be comfortable unless they had some sort of skeleton outline.

The Physical Appearance of Your Notes

The notes we've just been discussing for brainstorming are for instant use. Once they've served their purpose in helping you sort your ideas out you'll probably (though not necessarily) throw them in the wastebasket.

But what if you are writing notes that you expect to use again in the future? Then you need to consider their physical appearance on the page. The grotty appearance of many students' notes perhaps to the point of illegibility, may be one reason why they make less use of them later than they had originally expected.

Here are some questions to consider in relation to the layout and presentation of your own notes.

1 Do I always label my notes so as to show what they are about, where I got them from, and when I made them?

2 Can I read my own handwriting?

3 Have I worked out a set of abbreviations that I can use consistently *and* understand when I read them later!

4 Do I leave plenty of white space in and around my writing? (Narrow margins and tightly packed lines of writing squeezed together make pages of notes difficult to read, difficult to add to and difficult to remember - because one page looks much like another.)

5 Do I, for example, break up my material into digestible chunks by using, where possible:

lists (like this one)?

indentation (as here)?

numbered or lettered points?

headings and sub-headings?

boxes around important items?

6 Do I indicate the relative importance of various items by:

varying the size of my writing?

sometimes using CAPITALS?

underlining words and phrases?

using different coloured pens (with discretion)?

7 Do I use drawings or diagrams to capture ideas that cannot be so easily expressed in words and/or to make the page of notes more visually memorable?

If you cannot say 'yes', then you may need to look for ways of improving the legibility, layout and visual clarity of your notes. They don't have to be works of art, but do try to think of them in terms of graphic design. Each page makes a visual pattern and you should find it helpful in using the notes if each page presents a different pattern.

Professor Derek Rowntree. The Open University.

This chapter, taken from *Learn How to Study*, Macdonald London 1970, and published with permission of the copyright owner in *History Sixth*, issue 5, is reprinted here with the permission of the author and Little Brown, Great Dover Street, London.

3

The Essay

THE WRITING OF ESSAYS for Advanced Level and college is so usual a requirement that it has the force of tradition. In any case, that is how the subject is by and large examined, so that the one leads inevitably to the other. Yet many a weary student doing their weekly assignment or teacher faced with yet another pile of marking to blight the weekend, must on occasions wonder whether there are not simpler ways to develop and test historical knowledge. When one considers how hard some students work at producing their essays, the preparation and reading required before they even set pen to paper, the French prose or Shakespearean commentary seems almost a soft option. Meanwhile their teachers accept as part of their lot, the regular and conscientious scrutiny of twenty or more pieces, often on similar subjects, for which they must find time apart from their teaching and its preparation. A whole catalogue of errors, from factual inaccuracies to contradictory statements, poor grammar to worse judgements, circular arguments to spelling mistakes, have to be painstakingly itemised and amended, week in, week out; criticism has to be balanced with encouragement, justice with a good deal of imaginative mercy; given the burden that the average Advanced Level History teacher carries, what is remarkable is the high level of freshness and enthusiasm so many retain. That their students are the richer for it there can be no doubt, for in essay writing the student is learning his craft and, though not always immediately apparent, over a period of time develops a range of skills that is both historically and educationally useful. Indeed, cumulatively, the whole is greater than the sum of parts. A historical education, it must always be remembered, grows beyond the discipline's subject boundaries.

Pavlov-dog Syndrome

At its most basic the essay is a vehicle for setting out some ideas and information relating to a particular historical problem. A question has been asked and an answer of sorts must be provided. Since history is a complex subject at any serious level and few historical questions allow of a trite affirmative or negative response, the essay provides the necessary space for a sorting out of one's ideas and relaying of information relevant to the topic in hand. Ideas, of course, need direction and relevance implies selectivity; the essay writer has to marshal his facts and organise his arguments.

This, in turn, will be determined by the length of the essay and the breadth of the question. To make a stab at, say, explaining why the Reformation spread in sixteenth-century Europe in six pages or three-quarters of an hour is going to place a high premium on essential facts and clear-sighted arguments. Lady Gwendolen Cecil in her biography of the Marquess of Salisbury, the Victorian Prime Minister, recounts how he once said that making major decisions was no different from deciding whether to take his raincoat on a country walk. The same is true for a history essay. There are certain essential facts, the absence of which vitiates the whole argument; find these and the essay begins to write itself. The essay, of course, is not on automatic pilot; the operative word is 'begins'; but in answering a historical question, it is salutary to recall, the writer is following the truth not leading it.

Indeed, error more likely comes not from following truth, but from following it in the wrong direction. Many unsatisfactory essays are not in themselves poor pieces of work; they are inadequate because they do not answer the actual question set. It is the Pavlov-dog syndrome. Full of his knowledge of one particular topic, examination nerves or the desire to sock it to the essay reader, the student sees the magic words he is looking for, ignoring their context or qualifications. A question on the Alliance system before World War I becomes a question on the origins of the War itself; a question on Baldwin and the General Strike turns into a potted history of inter-war conservatism. Within ten sentences the writer is, metaphorically, over the hills and far away. Really this is an unnecessary error; unless the essay title is ambiguous, and this alas! does sometimes happen, the most humdrum student ought to be clear about what is actually asked.

Seeing the Obvious

So the essay writer at the outset has acquired a valuable skill - the need to ask what is intellectually required of him. This is by no means as commonplace as one might suppose. A few years ago, perhaps even now, a women's magazine ran an agony aunt column under the heading 'The Man Who Sees'. What was pretty readily apparent was that the correspondents often did not; a lot of the questions only arose because the questioners could not or perhaps would not see the obvious; that having affairs with married men in the office twice one's age was not likely to form the basis for lasting happiness or fiancés who lived in the local were unlikely to turn into model husbands. Once the right questions were asked, the answers fell into place. Common sense is alas! not that common. One can make too much of this but a training in asking the right question spills over into life as well as education. Not for nothing has history so often been the subject of politicians and administrators.

 Once the question is posed, next comes the task of meeting the challenge. For a particular question, what are the fundamental issues that must be confronted? What factors, though important, can be relegated to a secondary role? What facts or issues though valid can, if necessary, be ignored, passed over briefly or interred in a simple paragraph? Immediately the writer has moved into one of the most valuable of educational exercises, the need to assign priority, emphasis and value. This is not necessarily learned easily and its mastery distinguishes the good from the indifferent essay. Coupled with this intellectual ranking is its corollary, space and time. We have no doubt all erred in this direction; the over-long introduction, the three pages where three paragraphs would have sufficed, the hurried conclusion implicit rather than explicit from our argument as space and time ran out.

The Trap of Narrative

The assignment of emphasis and the arrangement of material, however, is but a means to an end; the answering of the question by the fashioning of an argument. This, it must be admitted, is not always obvious; and many a lacklustre essay falls into the trap of a narrative survey, a Cook's tour, as it were, of the historical information available to the author, rather than a direct response to the question set. It is this overarching purpose that makes or breaks an essay; a powerful, clear-sighted, cogent argument sweeps the material up in its path, a fusion of reason and information that aims to convince; whilst its poor relation flops at intervals, picking up the track again as another thought occurs, its contents not necessarily well-integrated, sometimes circular in approach or even contradictory. Muddled thinking leads to muddled writing; one purpose of the essay is to enable the writer to sift his thoughts and in so doing acquire a clearer understanding of the problem he is addressing.

The pursuit of truth sounds perhaps portentous but that is what the writing of an essay requires. But if the writer must think clearly, he must also write clearly; otherwise his argument may be misconstrued. And the pursuit of clarity of expression inevitably entails clarity of thought; the two are locked together in unyielding embrace. Historians, to take but one example, have spilled a lot of ink and no doubt perspiration on the concept of the gentry in seventeenth-century England and their putative rise or decline; clearly historical explanation requires an examination of concepts too lightly or too loosely used; 'bourgeoise', 'middle-class', 'revolution', 'crisis', to name but a few. A writer of a history essay has to be quite a canny individual, no bad thing as a form of intellectual training, ready to meet, indeed anticipate, objections to his arguments and knock them on the head.

Economy of Thinking

To prescribe clear thinking is easier than to practise it. Yet the challenge must be met and mastered. Logic, the ability to see the implications of one's statements, the willingness to accept inconvenient facts and not sweep them aside, the patient rigour involved in constructing a water-tight argument that leaves no hostages to fortune, power of analysis, depth of understanding, scepticism in the face of the plausible, the suspect or the trite, in essence that quality of reflective openness of mind that steers a middle course between prejudice and indecision, these are the salient attributes of a successful essay. No one who has perfected these virtues, often over a period of years, would doubt the efficacy of essay writing in producing the rational, thoughtful, fluent, incisive educated man or woman that properly results from a genuine historical education. Often, sadly, there is a gap between ideal and reality, and good habits are not carried over into ordinary life; but the fact remains that the history essay is, of its nature, the antithesis of the wild statement, unsubstantiated assertion, snide comment, prejudiced half-truth or hysterical head-line that alas! in a supposedly literate society forms much of the staple diet offered by the popular press to the general public as their sole reading matter.

For the essay is an exercise in self-discipline. Facts, not sentiment, dictate its bias. The writer learns that whilst he must master his material, he too must allow it to master him. He is the servant of his sources. Strong religious feelings he may have, but the facts of a case might compel him to admit that Christian churches could have propped up unsavoury regimes to the general detriment of their people; a fervent socialist, he may have to detail the excesses of revolutionaries and see that old orders are not necessarily replaced by something better. The essay writer learns that grey, not black or white, is likely to be the characteristic colouring of most human beings and their situations. Yet tolerance, albeit desirable, must not slip over into relativism or indifference. It is quite something, at the age, say, of seventeen to begin to make mature, considered, balanced judgements about people and events often far removed in time and place. To read dispassionately into the minds of, for example, the medieval Cathars, or investigate fairly the blunderings, near-misses, lucky strikes and lost opportunities that make up the history of European colonisation of the New World, is to develop an intellectual depth and generosity that is an immensely valuable mental and cultural attribute. To learn to summarise one's discoveries, to analyse, explore, question and interpret them, all within the strict framework the essay necessitates, is to practise that antidote to intellectual chaos, the ability to order and to arrange. Of course, the discipline can be circumvented; over-long, tedious, repetitive essays represent the failure of the writer to submit to his mandate; that economy of thought succeeds by its restraint, where diffuseness fails through its excess.

Golden Mouths

And thought on paper, is subject to the severest scrutiny. That great figure of the fourth-century Near-Eastern church St John earned the soubriquet Chrysostom (golden-mouthed) because of the fame of his preaching. Doubtless the title was well-deserved. Few essay writers, however, are likely to be so honoured. No golden words can charm away manifest illogic; pleasant phrases and too plausible arguments when spoken, face a sterner test read slowly and at leisure. The essay is remorseless in its detection of inconsistency. How does page five compare to the opening paragraph? Surely the writer said exactly the reverse four pages ago? How can that set of arguments lead to this conclusion? Why must the writer wander off the point for the best part of three pages? The criticism is chilling but hopefully constructive. It is no bad thing to keep one's wits about one and know that in the essay, at least, intellectual cheating, albeit unintentional, is unlikely to go unpunished.

Yet as Lincoln said at the height of the Civil War: 'The occasion is piled high with difficulty, and we must rise with the occasion'. The essay's format is a superb outlet for the resolution of historical truth. It does allow scope for intellectual independence; one can concentrate on the particular without ignoring the general. There is time to explore the minor matters as well as the major themes. One can both chance one's arm and hedge one's bets. Some writers favour a frontal assault on a problem; others are more circuitous in their approach. Any one who has had much experience of reading essays will confirm that students have an intellectual identity as much as personal or physical characteristics. There can be a genuine, disinterested pleasure in getting to know a good mind via the work it produces. And the students themselves, getting more confident in their powers by reason of constant practice, soon learn to tackle tougher assignments and master more complex material with literary feats that would have surprised themselves when they first began.

Two Hundred Per Cent Art

To say that essay writing develops character is redolent of cold baths and pre-breakfast jogging. Yet there is a sense in which the search for and arrangement of material, the tailoring of it to a particular need, the concentration required to see it through to its conclusion, the willingness to pause and examine where one has been and where one is going with one's argument, the ability, if facts dictate, to change one's mind, must help produce a more mature, balanced, well-rounded individual. The essay does require effort; there is such a thing as writer's block; one does have to get stuck-in to fashion some sort of answer; one does have to make up one's own mind on the evidence available; truth is not acquired without a certain sacrifice. Yet the rewards are well worth it. One comes to appreciate the aesthetics of intellectual inquiry; that truth is beautiful; that there is a particular appropriateness in an idea fittingly expressed. It is recounted of one very famous historian that as a schoolboy he wrote an essay on an examination paper that was wrong, but so brilliantly wrong that the examiner wanted to give him two hundred per cent! The story may be apocryphal but it does illustrate how the history essay writer has an opportunity denied many of his contemporaries, weighed down by the need to absorb and regurgitate vast amounts of mere knowledge, to express himself through his material; the prerogative of the artist through the ages.

Much energy has been expended on arguing whether history is an art or a science; perhaps the truth is, it has attributes of both. The possibility of intermeshing evidence with evaluation, judgement with objectivity, reason with insight, imagination with analysis, all attributes of the essay, suggests that amidst all the necessary drudgery and tedium, lies an opportunity for intellectual self-fulfilment that affords both utility and pleasure. Mathematicians, it is rumoured, distinguish between solutions to problems that are adequate and those that are elegant. The history-essay writer shares this potential but on a wider canvas. Yet his subject matter is, ultimately, human beings and their doings. He breathes life into the departed. There can be few acts of creativity its equal.

John Kentleton. Liverpool University.

4

Essay Planning: Early Steps

THE ARRIVAL OF A STUDENT in the sixth form is fraught with a number of intimidating novelties and one of these is essay writing. An Advanced Level essay can be an ordeal because the student has had limited experience of essay work.

I hope to show in this article that essay writing need not be too onerous and that the process of preparing an essay can be also a valuable aid to learning and preparation for examinations. Teachers regard the writing of essays as a skill rather akin to learning to ride a bike: keep at it and eventually you will get it right! Some people have the idea that either you can write essays or you cannot and if you can't you will never learn the knack. This article is aimed at helping those that can write essays to write better ones and those who find it difficult to find a way that they can use to begin to develop effective essay preparation.

Fast-track Organisation

The first guideline is to set up a kind of scaffolding or skeleton on which to hang the flesh of the essay. It may seem unduly inflexible but I recommend a constant nine paragraphs for all essays.

Paragraph 1 should be an introduction to the essay. It could give a few background details but you should then turn to outlining the main topics you will cover in the essay. In this way it can be seen as a sort of plan, albeit written out in full sentences. To write this introduction you need to look carefully at the title and work out exactly what it is asking you for.

Consider, for example, this essay title: 'How were the seven northern provinces of the Netherlands able to achieve their independence by 1609?'

The date is very important because it specifies a particular point and that you should be aware of it and make reference to it.

As is well known, examiners will give only a low grade to even a good narrative of the events. To achieve a higher grade there must be some analysis. In the introduction you should point out the six main factors that led to Dutch independence. Each factor then becomes the subject of one of the paragraphs in the body of the essay.

Paragraphs 2-7 should deal with these six factors - one by one. In your planning, before you start to write, you should identify six main factors. For this essay I could suggest:

2 Religion
3 Finance
4 William of Orange
5 Spanish mistakes
6 Military reforms
7 Geographical influences

You may think that it is better to emphasise Spanish distractions or foreign help and base a paragraph on these. Your teachers might well prefer to include other factors but I am sure that you should select six main reasons/headings and fit others around these. It is a discipline to always make yourself think of six main headings for any topic. Returning to use the method, for the modern period, consider this example: 'Why did the Bolsheviks win the civil war? The subject for paragraphs 2-7 for this essay could be:

2 Military reasons
3 Quality of leadership
4 Economic reasons
5 Weaknesses of the White opposition
6 Nationalism
7 Strategic and geographical influences

In each paragraph you should make clear points. For instance, religion was an important reason for resistance to the Spanish.

You must then go on to provide clear EVIDENCE to back up the point you have made. This can be repeated a number of times in the paragraph, but you should also try to develop the point; to look for the implications of what you have said. We can say this is making a comment on the point. There is then a formula for each paragraph; POINT, EVIDENCE, COMMENT. Some of the evidence might not be in agreement with the theme of your answer but you have an opportunity to deal with that problem afterwards. In fact, it is a good idea to show two different versions of what the events might mean and examiners give credit for this approach especially where you show awareness of the historiography of a topic and indicate this knowledge in your answer.

Paragraph 8 is the discussion section. The aim in this part of the essay is to look at all the factors and weigh their importance. You might need to argue the strength of some factors against others or question the significance of some of the evidence. This leads you on to the final paragraph which is:

Paragraph 9 The conclusion. This is where you give the answer to the question asked in the title. The conclusion should be quite brief and to the point.

Notice that the tail end of the essay has developed two paragraphs where you might have been told to write only one - the conclusion. This is to force you to include both the aims of the conclusion: to discuss and argue the factors in the question and also to write a firm answer.

Course Essays

The method described above can be used for course essays. To gain maximum benefit you should plan the essay first, do the extra necessary reading, write what notes you need and then try to write the whole essay in one go inside two hours. With a time restriction, your teacher would have to be in agreement that your essay was not going to stand any chance of being a twenty page masterpiece and of course you might lose some of the benefits of deep and wide reading but it is to be hoped that you will gain in focus.

Your reading and research will have definite aims and the notes you write will be focused on answering the question. It makes your time management easier and prevents the writing of an essay from seeming to require such an 'Everest effort', a thought that daunts even the willing student. This approach to writing and preparing essays also provides an opportunity for your teachers to help you in selecting the relevant factors - you are both aiming at the same objective. This can make the lesson that follows a topic particularly valuable as it can be used as an essay preparation session involving inquiry, assessment of factors and discussion.

Essay Preparation and Revision

The basic approach can be adapted to fit different types of essay. For instance you might have an essay that asks you to develop an argument. Here you can adjust the method to write three paragraphs looking at one side of the question and the second three main body paragraphs looking at the other side of the question. The discussion section then provides the area to argue one side against the other. You can also look at a number of factors and assess them in each paragraph, weighing the evidence in the discussion section.

Both during the course and at its end you will have to prepare for examinations. The best way to do this is to look at past questions and identify the main types of questions that occur. Write essay plans for them and research them in depth. This problem solving approach to revision is more stimulating than the traditional page after page memorising method and helps you avoid falling into the trap of writing the dreaded narrative answer. The skill of revising then transfers to the skill of answering examination questions. Once again the management of your time is enhanced and the activity is more active and more interesting.

The final area of guidance is related to the question of time. History students in many Advanced Level examinations are allowed only forty-five minutes to write an answer. I suggest that you think and plan for about three minutes and then use about three minutes to write the introduction. The six main body paragraphs should each take five minutes, as should the discussion section, leaving just a couple of minutes to write a short but punchy conclusion. In other words, this procedure helps you to monitor your use of examination time and to pace yourself.

Evaluating the Procedure

The argument against this method is that it is rather mechanical, but in its favour it does provide a means of helping students with a clearly defined approach to a task that they often find very difficult.

The most useful aspect of this method is that it teaches students to structure their essays very carefully and provides a framework for constructive critical discussion with teachers and fellow students. The essay writers should know what they are trying to achieve at each stage in the essay and it becomes easier to point out where students are going wrong in a way that they can understand and so try to remedy.

Students have developed the method to help them structure much longer pieces of work and a surprising number of essays by students I have taught, submitted at college and university have received praise for their strong organisation. Effective structure makes a strong answer much more likely and enhances the chances of a good grade.

Michael Slattery. Cotham Grammar School, Bristol.

Further Steps with Essay Work

ADVANCED LEVEL WORK, compared to GCSE work, requires a different approach. Your organisation, application and motivation are more important. You will have, probably, some choice with the texts you can use. You are encouraged to develop individual methods, skills and approaches to work that suit you and that are effective. These skills include the management, including the pacing, of work assignments and the development of skills with reading, including scanning and information extraction, as well as effective note making.

As an Advanced Level student you will be encouraged to develop a sense of period and a deeper understanding of the influences and personalities of your period. This will be helped by the reading and noting that you complete in addition to class work, as well as by discussion, either formal or informal, with your fellow students and with your teachers - discussion in which ideas are expressed and exchanged. Reflection and thought in relation to your reading is valuable and essays, in particular, challenge this.

An Essay of Quality

A good essay answer will reflect your preparation. Much of this can be described as routine work. A good essay answer will indicate a sound understanding of the topic, an understanding that is based upon thorough reading and thoughtfulness about that which is read and it will show that you have assimilated the information and ideas for the topic by your ability to effectively use information.

Your answer can be seen, also, as a measure of your use of your intellectual ability - your brain power. It will be evident by:

- Your understanding of the meaning of the question and its implications.

- Your ability to direct your information to the question that is asked.

- Your ability to plan and order your answer.

Michael Slattery describes and discusses his method for essay preparation, a method that he has used to help many students, in the previous article. Initial essay work may be depicted as substantially technical and mechanical; the essay becomes a 'patchwork', a 'cut and paste' product of statements, ideas and information from the texts and monographs from which the student made notes while the better essays, in addition, will refer to particular, named, historians and their interpretations and views.

Do not forget that your plan should be an analysis: that is, your essay plan is based on *your statements, evaluations and arguments* and it should not be merely a summary of information. Needless to say, your statements, evaluations and arguments will be based upon your information on the topic but an essay ordered directly round information will tend to follow an undemanding narrative or story pattern.

The Next Step: Individuality

When student essay writers move up to 'the premier league' they become more thoughtful and critical as they read and they incorporate into notes *their thoughts, reactions, observations and questions* about what they read. These thoughts and questions *are used to guide further reading.*

While essays remain structured, ordered, focused on the question, carefully and clearly expressed and with examples to illustrate and support statements they also - when the next step is taken - become the channel for the presentation of the student's own views and thoughts. The essay will become less 'cut and paste', but instead the unique, the singular, product of a reflective thinker. The essay writer will be more like a sculptor or a potter who, in response to the material (wood, clay or historical information), crafts an individual work that reflects the mind, the personality and the ideas of the craftsman-creator. The essay ceases to be an object mechanically fitted together and made but an individual creation.

Students should feel confident that their views and reflections, as long as they are well founded on historical evidence as summarised in monographs and textbooks, and as long as they are not too eccentric and palpably implausible, because they are indications of thought, are welcomed by those who assess essays.

Gilbert Pleuger.

5

Style

Whoever thinks a faultless piece to see
Thinks what ne'er was, nor is, nor e'er shall be.

SO WROTE ALEXANDER POPE in his *Essay on Criticism* in the
mid-eighteenth century. In modern terms, Pope is saying that
however well an examination answer, for example, is written, it
will always fall short of the ideal.

Even if this gives you, as an examination candidate, some
comfort, you will probably want to get as close to the ideal as
you can. So how can you improve your *style?* How can you
convey your ideas in the best possible manner to the examiner?

The Writer and the Reader

In answering this rhetorical question, some consideration of the
examiner himself is perhaps an appropriate starting point. What
sort of creature is he? What is he looking for in an answer? What
pleases him? What annoys him? What generalisations can we
make about the men and women who set your examination
papers, and then mark them?

Well, most examiners are busy people with a few hundred
scripts to mark. They are likely to be pushed for time - the
quicker they can get through a paper, the sooner they will be
finished! So make things easier for them. If your hand-writing is
clear, their task is easier. Even on this basic level, your means of
expression can affect the examiner's disposition towards you.

And try to make your answers interesting. Don't be a bore! A bore tells you everything, whether you already know it or not. Writing about Second World War strategy, for example, do not write

> *Churchill broadcast to the British people, 'Never in the history of human endeavour was so much owed by so many to so few'.*

The examiner surely knows this. Try instead to *allude* to the speech with some such words as:

> *Churchill's tribute to 'the few' stressed the dependence of the country on its first line of defence, the RAF fighter pilots.*

Quoting 'the few' shows that you know the speech: but you have also made a point about defence priorities. And in giving consideration to what it is reasonable to expect the examiner to take for granted, you are more likely to maintain his interest.

And then there is the question of what might be called the *level* from which you should address the examiner. Should you talk down to him? Should you address him on equal terms? Or should you write as if he was a superior being? After all, he must have more knowledge than you; otherwise he would not be where he is.

By and large, address him as an equal. In your answers you are frequently trying to explain things or persuade him to accept your point of view by means of rational argument backed up by evidence. The fact that you *reason* with someone implies that you are treating him as an equal. You probably adopt this tone with your friends when trying to convince them of your point of view. To people whom you consider inferior or superior to yourself (if such people exist) you might be dogmatic or subservient.

Some phrases which characterise the different tones of address are shown below:

	CHARACTERISTICS	TYPICAL PHRASES
Talking down	God-like omniscience	You must understand . . .
		There is no question but that . . .
	Unduly forceful	Undoubtedly . . .
	Dogmatic	If you accept that you will accept . . .

continued overpage

	CHARACTERISTICS	TYPICAL PHRASES
On an equal footing	Good manners Consideration for the reader Civilised conversation	It is reasonable to assume that . . . It would be unwise to give too much weight to X's views . . . It may be recalled that . . . It is, perhaps, an overstatement to say . . . It seems . . . It would appear that . . .
Subservient	Obsequious Unduly diffident	If I might suggest . . . My opinion, for what it is worth . . .

The phrases illustrating 'talking down' and 'subservient' are caricatures, but they help to make a point. You are writing for someone whom you must assume to be knowledgeable, reasonable, and who will consider arguments backed up by evidence; he may, however, be impatient and he is in any case accustomed to views being expressed according to certain conventions. So let us now look at some of the features which characterise acceptable academic argument.

Use of the Personal Pronoun, I

It is wise to avoid the use of the first person. To write *I think . . ., I do not agree that . . .* and so on is generally regarded as the intrusion of an overly subjective note into what should be an objective answer. Examiners usually prefer an impersonal approach.

Even if you are asked if you agree with a statement, or to what extent something is true, your view should be expressed in such phrases as *it seems . . ., one might say that . . .,* or *it could be argued that . . .* These are acceptable ways of giving your own opinion, without bringing yourself into the picture to any great extent.

To illustrate this, here are two versions of the same material:

1 *I would call Wagner a subjective artist. What I mean is that his art had its source in his personality. I find his work virtually independent of the epoch in which he lived.*

2 *Wagner was what might be called a subjective artist in that his art had its source in his personality. His work seems virtually*

independent of the epoch in which he lived.

Both versions express the same view. Both express the view of the writer. In the first version, however, the writer is in the forefront: the reader's attention is diverted *from* his subject *to* the writer. Good manners require that you stand back when expressing your opinions. Hence the impersonal phrases.

Jargon and Cliché

Avoid the use of jargon and cliché. Having been over-used, their meanings have become imprecise. Here is an example of jargon:

> The statutes covering education grant parental choice of schools so long as accommodation is available. Unfortunately, over a period of time, the schools in this Borough, because of the highly residential area and increasing housing development, have experienced difficulties with accommodation . . .

This is bureaucratic jargon. Phrases like *parental choice* and *housing development* and words like *statutes, accommodation* and *available* flow fluently from the pens of bureaucrats. The individual words are unnecessarily long: the writer seems to be trying to impress one with his own cleverness rather than get his message across as simply as possible.

The following passage tells parents what they need to know without jargon:

> Parents have the right to choose their children's school so long as there is room. Unfortunately, over some years, pressure on places has increased greatly because of the number of new houses built.

Overtones

Some words are so embued with overtones that they appeal more to the emotions of the reader than to his reason. Overleaf are three groups of words, used more often because of their emotional appeal than because of their basic meaning. Words in the first group trigger off positive responses: their users intend you to be influenced favourably by them. The second group of words provoke negative responses.

Words with overtones of approval	Words with overtones of disapproval	Words whose overtones depend on the user's views or on the context
flexible	rigid	defensive
sophisticated	escalation	work-ethic
stimulating	bureaucratic*	discriminate
challenging	monolithic	middle-class
educational	authoritarian	
commitment		
imaginative		
professional		

* What was your reaction to this word
when you read it in the previous section?
It was intended to gain your disapproval!

Let us look closely at the use of one of these words: challenging. In a challenging job, you will presumably need to use all your wits and strength. Challenging has thus come to have the opposite meaning to boring. Employers advertise jobs as challenging in order to attract people who are seeking job-satisfaction. Both employer and employee assume that a challenging job is a good job. The word has gained an overtone of approval.

It can, however, be overdone. If every job is described as challenging, applicants will become more wary. They will come to realise that so-called challenging jobs are just difficult, dirty and possibly under-paid ones. They will tend to avoid them!

In academic essays, think hard about the overtones of the words you use. Don't use words merely for their emotive appeal. You are not writing speeches for politicians, or copy for the tabloid press! You are writing for a discriminating reader - the examiner - who has been trained to be very precise in his choice of words so that he can convey a precise meaning to his reader.

As an exercise, you might like to group the following words in the three categories to show the overtones they convey:

aggressive, articulate, assertive, chronic, compromise, confront, consultation, defensive, dogma, educational, feed-back, formal, hierarchy, immigrant, informal, inimitable, manipulative, monitor, motivation, negative, open-ended, sensitive, supportive, systematic, therapeutic, typical, viable, working-class.

The fact that you may find it hard to decide which category some words belong to, may help to convince you of the need for careful choice and definition!

Sentence Structure

Particularly in analytical writing, one tends to use long, involved sentences. One is expressing complex ideas, and one's style becomes correspondingly complex.

Try not to let your sentences ramble wildly. One method of pruning them is to cut out dependent clauses (containing finite verbs), substituting phrases (governed by the infinitive or by participles) instead. Look at the following sentence:

> The standard of living, *which was already higher in America than in England,* continued to rise because people were able to use large-scale machinery *which was economical on the prairies but would have been uneconomical in the small English fields.*

This sentence makes its point more swiftly if well pruned. The two relative clauses (in italic type) can be shortened into phrases:

> The standard of living, *already higher in America than in England,* continued to rise because people were able to use large-scale machinery *economical on the prairies but not in the small English fields.*

Looked at another way, the finite verbs, *were, was,* and *would have been,* have been removed.

Always have an eye to brevity. You should have a lot of points to make, examples to give, and ideas to express. Develop as taut a style as possible so as to get the important things down on paper quickly.

Meaningful Verbs

One more small point of style can liven up your answers considerably. This involves the use of meaningful verbs.

The verbs *to be* and *to have* are over-used in analytical writing. Two examples from the American space programme illustrate this:

> 'We have touch-down' means 'The space vehicle has landed'.

> 'We have deployment of drogues' means 'The parachutes have opened'.

In both cases a static situation - 'touch-down' or 'deployment of drogues' is said to exist. In grammatical terms, one can say that *nouns* are being used in place of *verbs*. The idea of movement (landing and opening) has been lost and this lack of movement can be boring.

Try to use meaningful verbs in place of static phrases. Instead of writing 'We are in a class-contact situation', consider whether 'We *are being taught*' would not express the idea more accurately. Or do you really mean 'We *are taking* notes' or 'We *are discussing* Elizabeth I'? If so, say so.

Again, if you feel like writing 'In 1918 there was a resolution of the conflict', ask yourself whether 'The conflict *was resolved* in 1918' would be more appropriate. The verbs (in italic type) of both second versions pack more punch than those of the originals.

In a short article of this kind, there is only room to deal with a few of the many points which go to make up *style*. What lies behind all that has been touched on is the idea that one is writing for a particular reader, the examiner. Apart from testing your knowledge of your subject matter and your ability to reason, he is looking for clarity of expression - what Pope would have called 'wit':

> *True wit is nature advantage dress'd*
>
> *What e'er was thought but ne'r so well express'd.*

Christopher Moor.

Thinking for Yourself

WHEN I WAS AT SCHOOL my history teacher used to urge us to bring originality to our essays. We were not very good at this and part of the reason was our uncertainty as to what he meant.

Mission Impossible?

The most direct way to be original is to consider primary sources or, better still, find new primary sources. Leroy Ladurie used the hitherto neglected records of the Inquisition in his study that was later to be published as *Montaillou*. The book is a sharp illustration of the influence of primary sources on a well-worked period of history. Sixth formers do not have access to rich collections of documents and even the heavily selected and edited printed collections available to them are barely adequate to fulfil this role.

Now that I'm older I think my history teacher when he enjoined us to be original wanted us to take a fresh look at the topic and avoid a heavy dependence upon the class texts. He did not want our essays to be entirely derivative from our books, a sort of cut and paste of textbook statements. In particular he wanted us to free ourselves from the evaluations and generalisations in the texts.

Beefburgers Need Beef

How can an A Level student have an individual, a fresh, view on a topic? How can any statement be other than taken from a printed source? Most students would agree that their study is a constant battle with deadlines. Hardly is one assignment or essay completed before another deadline is set. Study readily alternates between reading and noting followed by essay work. Certainly reading, understanding and noting is one cornerstone of the history student's work and assignment and essay work is another but between these two is another cornerstone - reflection on the information. This stage is often skipped because, when under pressure of time, it is possible to deliver an assignment or essay without it. If, however, the middle stage is included into the work programme, tendencies toward a weak 'cut and paste' essay are reduced and at the same time the middle stage increases the value of stage one (reading and noting), raises the standard of stage three (written assignment and essay work) and heightens your mastery, and therefore enjoyment, of the topic. The best bit of a burger is the beef: to neglect it is a waste.

Workout with Information:

To gain more advantage from notes they should not be created only as a summary and record of ideas and information for an assignment or essay - thereafter to be filed away until unearthed for revision for an examination - but as a resource for further work before the essay is written. At the simplest, this work could be the creation of a chronology, preferably on one sheet of A4, to clarify the sequence of events. A chronology that is arranged by areas of activity or institution will help an understanding of the relations and/or interconnections between events. Secondly, the main influences on a situation, scientists call these the variables, can be identified and represented diagrammatically by an ideas map. Further, people and events are understood more fully if they are placed within the contemporary social and political and/or administrative structure and (when appropriate) given geographical location on a map. Finally, when notes are lengthy, an abstract of the chief arguments will help understanding. These notes made from notes, together with chronology and diagrams, made when the reading is still fresh in the mind, will provide the core information when you revise. Much of this activity is not demanding - less demanding than learning or writing an essay -

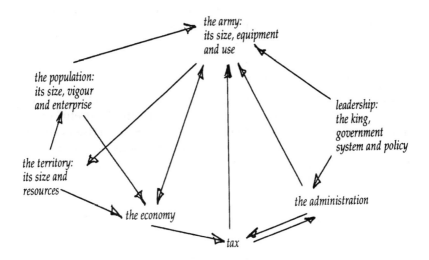

but time set aside for it enables you to gain some detachment from the roller coaster of information while also it enables greater understanding and perspective.

While reworking first draft notes you will identify questions the answers to which will more fully explain the events. These questions will be the focus for further reading, lead by indexes and chapter headings and sub-headings, when time allows.

Power Tools

If you are more enterprising you will further reduce your dependence on textbooks for analysis and generalisations. By the application of a schema for analysis you can produce your own ideas and generalisations and examples of schema for the power of a state and the strength of a ruler in early-modern Europe are shown below.

The Power of States

1 *Natural Advantages of the State.* Size, soil, climate, minerals, population, position.

2 *Opportunities for the Society and the State.* Agriculture, industry, communication (internal/external), trade, administrative, fiscal and financial institutions, military skills, technological innovation.

3 *Problems within Society and for the State.* Wealth creation (management of the economy); administrative management; political and/or social discontent/concord; natural disasters (drought, floods . . .).

4 *The influence of other States.*

In discussion with fellow students, inside or outside class, you can decide on other schema for analysis. A particularly useful one is 'Influences on a ruler's/stateman's power'. Some History books, such as the General History of Europe series, published by Longman, or Christopher Hill's *The Century of Revolution,* because their arrangement is thematic make this easier.

Dungeons and Dragons

Academic historians avoid hypothetical questions in their accounts of the past but hypothetical questions can be a   stepping-stone to greater understanding. Students may find what might loosely be called 'exercises' with widely known standard information on a topic a prompt to see a topic with fresh eyes.

Student games where all participants are winners.

- Isolate the main elements and considerations in a historical situation or, to use the scientist's phrase, create a model of the situation. Now vary one of the elements and see how the others are affected. *Try this with reasons for Spanish decline in the seventeenth century (see diagram on page forty-nine).*

- Change the order of events and assess the probable consequences - NB, this is especially useful where the events changed occurred within a short period and had marked consequences. *Example: Russia's acceptance of negotiations with Austria on 1 August 1914 after the German decision for war on Russia. Exchange the order. Would subsequent events have been different? Why/why not?*

- Remove one or two juxtapositioned events and estimate the possible direction of events. *Example: remove the expulsion of the Sea Beggars on Elizabeth's orders from Dover (in 1572).*

- Assume some important project/aim that succeeded had failed (or that failed, had succeeded). Assess the consequences. *Examples: Thomas Wyatt's rising led to the capture of London, 1554, or Cavour failed to make an agreement with Napoleon III in 1859.*

In the light of your thoughts during the exercises reconsider the accepted interpretations. You should re-assess also the significance of people and events.

Picturing the Past

The students' study of history will have more vitality if they are able to 'see' the topic studied not as a 'book past' - words on the pages of a book about the past - but as a past that was real. Real for the people who were at the centre of events or who were affected by events. However remote the period, whether 50 years, 150 years or 500 years, every student has access to understanding the unchanging core of history, namely human nature. The feelings, fears and hopes of a sixteenth-century mercenary in Italy are qualitatively the same as those of a contemporary soldier. After all, the fear of death does not change whether the weapons are pikes or missiles and the nature of the pursuit of power, by influence over people and/or institutions, remains the same whether in the seventeenth century or the twentieth even if the institutions have changed in the twentieth century.

So I think my History teacher was right: we could have thought for ourselves far more than we did. History is a good medium to develop the capacity for individual thought: its development is not opposed to your skills as a historian but brings vitality, interest and excitement to your work and meanwhile it helps you on your way to a top grade.

Gilbert Pleuger.

7 —————————————————

Historical Analysis

THE STEP UP IN STANDARD from GCSE to A Level is very marked. Greater emphasis upon essay work, greater pupil self-direction and more intensiveness and thoroughness of study are just a few of the ways in which A Level work is more demanding. More fundamentally, GCSE may be characterised as focused on evidential, evaluative, descriptive and communication skills while Advanced Level study may be characterised as requiring the skills of analysis and synthesis and thus the capacity to identify categories (or factors) and select events into categories. Clearly, success for the student at Advanced Level requires greater intellectual power than GCSE work and it is right that this is the case because the student is two years closer to adulthood.

The new intellectual environment into which the unready GCSE-trained A Level student is placed can be a reason for confusion and dismay during the earlier months and high achievements at GCSE is limited preparation for the important A Level study tasks - identification of cause and consequence or, in other words, identification of interaction, and the need for care with relevance and selectivity which is associated with the writing of focused answers to evaluative questions.

Signposts for the Organisation of Information

To help the pupil meet these demands and keep a confident course in the sea of densely-packed information a method for the analysis of historical information is a major help and the methods used by three thinkers are used as a guide. Francis Bacon, René Descartes and Thomas Hobbes were central to increasing awareness about the scientific method during its early days in modern times. Three tasks are central to the scientific method: analysis or the identification and separation of the components of a situation; synthesis or the bringing together of separate items to form a composite (and integrated) whole and the skills, common to both operations, of identification, classification and selection.

Francis Bacon, 1561-1626, was Lord Chancellor to James I but also a profound student of thought. He reflected on how Man thinks and how we can find out about the world as it really is. He claimed syllogistic logic (for example: 'I am a father. All fathers are male. Therefore I am male') which was important in Aristotelian thought was unable to add significantly to our knowledge of the world and he was unsatisfied by the place of axioms (given principles, not open to examination) in Platonism. Bacon was also critical of Empiricists, those who hold that sound knowledge of the world can be gained only from our sense experience - he likened them to ants who tirelessly yet aimlessly collect data - as well as the 'spiders' of thought, the Rationalist thinkers who believed by the use of reason alone truths about the world could be discovered. Bacon wrote that Man, in the search for truth, had been too readily diverted by Idols, of which there were four kinds; Idols of the Tribe, Idols of the Den, Idols of the Market Place and Idols of the Theatre. Loosely speaking, these Idols represent Man's over-readiness to generalise and his unreliability with evidence, Man's tendency to individual and idiosyncratic thought, muddled thought as a consequence of the ill use of words and the danger of the acceptance of 'schools' of thought.

Bacon saw method as the key to the attainment of real knowledge of the world and the method he proposed in *Novum Organum*, 1620, involved the collection of information and the systematic creation of tables or lists of qualities - when qualities are present, when absent and the degree of the quality. If, for example, the reason for heat is to be found, the table of all known instances of the presence of heat will be made, then a table of instances of the absence of heat as well as a table to record the degree of heat. From these tables, coincidences can be identified and an interpretation or, in Bacon's words, a 'first vintage' made.

The Frenchman René Descartes, 1596-1650, who lived in the

Netherlands for most of his adult life, was similarly distrustful of the widely accepted 'truths' of the ancients and Descartes, like Bacon, saw the method to be the sure way to certainty of knowledge. This method he described in his books *Discourse on Method*, 1637, and *Meditations on the First Philosophy*, 1641. René Descartes wrote that the essence of natural science was relationship and relationship could be mathematically expressed. He saw extension, whether in the form of shape, position, motion or number, as the only necessary quality of matter whereas colour, sound, odour, taste, degree of hardness are secondary qualities and of these we can have little certainty because our ideas of these are confused and unclear.

The lifetime of the Englishman Thomas Hobbes coincided with the troubled and turbulent time of the Civil War and Interregnum. Thomas Hobbes spent most of his time in employment in the service of the Cavendish family, often as tutor, the head of which was the Earl of Devonshire. Like Bacon and Descartes, he saw method as the key to the attainment of knowledge and like them he had little time for schools of thought. Hobbes's greatest work, *Leviathan*, was published in 1651, in his later life, while he was in exile in Paris. Reality, he wrote, lay beneath the appearance that is derived from the senses. To comprehend this reality phenomenon should be analysed and separated into their simplest components then they can be reconstructed into an intelligible pattern. Although Hobbes made a contribution to the theory of knowledge, he is included here for his understanding of the psychology and motivations of men. Hobbes saw Mankind as willing to accept government because fear of death or injury at the hands of fellow men made it prudent to do so. Men, claimed Hobbes, were driven by appetites and desires and it was these that constrained Man's actions. Mankind, Hobbes gloomily thought, was by nature aggressive and socially reasonable only by need and rational only with practice.

These three thinkers, Bacon, Descartes and Hobbes, provide a step toward a method of teaching historical analysis in the classroom. Pupil progress is challenged by the teacher, through example, to achieve attainment with this difficult enterprise - namely, the analysis and synthesis of a historical topic. At its most basic, a topic is divided and re-divided into factors and phases. At this simple level, factors and phases may be envisaged as represented by the axis of a graph. The factors represent the main influences or forces behind events and these forces are sometimes located in institutions or corporations: sometimes they are expressed by personalities. With a marked shift or change of situation a new phase may be said to begin and in this later phase the forces, and their relationship with each other will be differently patterned, if only in a small way. Factors and phases analysis helps reveal the interactions of influences and helps toward an understanding of the forces behind the events. Events are seen, hereby, as the surface signs, the uneven surface above the turbulent currents below. The identification of the main forces of a situation, the factors, and the dynamic nature of history, its phases, enables the pupil to reform the past in his/her head but still 'populate' the past with the events as faithfully recounted in the textbooks. Now, however, the pupil pictures the past as a moving mechanism of power behind the rotating hands on the clockface of the past.

Three examples are offered to illustrate the process that has been described. Although drawn from early-modern European history the student of modern history will, nevertheless, appreciate the working of the process.

PHASES / FACTORS	1 The nobles revolt	2 Calvin- ist rising	3 Rebels gain a base	4 Divi- sions harden	5 Spanish power revival	6 Spanish diver- sions	7 Maurice consoli- dates
Date	1560-2	1566-8	1572-6	1576-9	1583-86	1586-93	1593-07
a. Social groups involved.							
b. Issues.							
c. Leaders on both sides.							
d. Political or military action.							
e. Military events: land or sea and geo- location.							
f. Role of religion.							
g. Third power involvement							
h. Spanish/rebel resources.							
j. Spanish priorities.							

Illustration 1: The Dutch Rebellion, 1560-1609.

PHASES / ASPECTS	1505-12 Monk	1512-17 Luther and 'salvation'	1517-21 Indulgencies and Rome	1521-22 Ban of Empire, Wartburg Bible	1522-29 Reform leader	1529-46 Church leader
Interpretation of the Bible						
Theology esp. eucharist and sacraments						
Theological authority						
Liturgy						
Role of priests						
Attitude to secular powers						
Church organisation						

Illustration 2: Aspects of Luther's thought and influence, 1505-1546. With this example factors are replaced by Luther's views and influence.

PHASES / FACTORS	1. 1589-10 Henri IV and Sully	2. 1610-17 Marie de Medici & Concini	3. 1617-24 Louis XIII and Luynes	4. 1624-42 Richelieu	5. 1642-48 Mazarin (I)	6. 1648-53 The two Frondes	7. 1653-61 Mazarin (II)	8. 1661-83 Louis XIV and Colbert
Crown								
Court								
Nobles								
Huguenots								
Catholics								
Council								
Central Govt								
Parlement								
Finance								
Economy								
Army & Navy								
Foreign								

Illustration 3: Changes in French Monarchical Power, 1589-1683.

It is pointless to disguise the difficulty of historical analysis. Some pupils will fail to achieve this for themselves at all, others will understand the process and make some headway only very late in their course while others will achieve a degree of mastery with the process but nevertheless make mistakes.

Factors and Phases and the Active Mind of the Student

The factors and phases method of teaching and understanding analysis is a way to teach history, to take events from a huge undifferentiated ragbag of happenings and to place them in a pigeon-hole structure: to identify and assess the main influences present in a situation. It is an approach which requires the pupil to actively organise and thereby to form the information - in his/her own mind - into a more manageable form. Once done, the factors and phases of a topic will be the main body of any essay on the topic, even if the arrangement will vary. It is not a rigid method and it can be employed in a variety of ways. And it does not claim to fully portray the past as it really was, that is too demanding an enterprise for a young mind, but to synthesise the past in a way that entertains the mind of an activated pupil because, above all, a factors and phases approach is suited to the classroom as a way to teach and a way to learn. For just as the musician uses the structure of treble and bass bars in written music on which to write notes, but the bars themselves are inaudible and not part of the music and are the creation of the writer, so too the pupil is helped by categories and classes which lead to an understanding beyond the story of the past.

Progress with historical analysis, once attained, will enable the student to play 'games of interpretation' (see, for example, the suggestions in Thinking for Yourself, *History Review* Supplement, December 1992, page 2) and participate more readily in discussions on interpretation. After all, History is pre-eminently a discipline given to debate, as Sir Geoffrey Elton reminds us. Lastly, it need hardly be mentioned, a pupil that has made even limited progress with historical analysis will tackle the more demanding evaluative and interpretative coursework and examination questions with greater competence and will have entered more fully into the study of the past.

This article was written by the Editor from notes made by Michael Barlen, author of Foundations of Modern Europe, 1968, *and Head Master of Bedford School, who died suddenly in the Swiss Alps in September 1991. It is published to commemorate an inspiring and gifted colleague and teacher to generations of students.*

8

How to Manage with Time

I WAS IN A STUDENT COFFEE BAR during my first week at university soaking in the atmosphere when a lad from Oldham of conspicuously cool and languid manner, announced that he intended to get a first in Classics. He would work 25 hours a week, study five hours a day on weekdays and leave the weekends free. That would be sufficient.

I was vaguely committed to endless hours of work. I imagined that at some point I would spend weeks of intensive study. The vice-chancellor had told us in his address to freshers to look at the person on either side and note that in all probability one of us would not be around the following year. The message struck home: I would turn myself into a paragon of academic virtue. I could see that the classicist in the coffee bar had got it all wrong, or was bluffing.

Three years later he sailed to his first whilst other friends struggled to very modest achievements. As I discovered when sharing his lodgings, he worked more or less to the plan he had outlined. He slept late in the mornings, only stirring himself if there was a lecture to attend. He played cards with the rest of us after lunch. Then he moved to his desk and stayed there till around seven. The evenings he spent more wildly than most - hence the late mornings.

A Modest but Well-defined Plan

Nevertheless, when I came to look back I realised he had studied more than anyone else I knew. Through sticking assiduously to a modest but well-defined, realistic plan, he had achieved a great deal. He had enjoyed work much more, too.

He argued that it was not possible to work productively at intensive intellectual tasks for more than a few hours at a time. I aimed to do much more. But I was easily distracted. By the time it was apparent that stretches of day had slipped away, I felt so guilty that I blotted studies out of my mind comforting myself with the thought of all the days which lay ahead.

I was too inexperienced at looking after my own affairs to realise I was already failing one of the major tests of studenthood, the organisation of time. I thought that success in studying was to do with how brilliantly clever and original you were; I had yet to discover that one of the central challenges of adult life is time management.

At school the work timetable was defined for us and teachers made sure we fitted all that was required into the school year. At university I was at sea. Time came in great undifferentiated swathes. What to do with it all? With 168 hours in a week - or 105, allowing nine a day for sleeping and eating - how many was it reasonable to spend on study? Individuals vary and different subjects make different demands. Nevertheless, with a target you can plan your studies, not just stumble ahead in hope. The sketchiest of weekly timetables, setting aside 40 hours to cover all study, is an invaluable aid in defining time. Then you can divide it into segments and use it strategically, rather than let it dribble away.

Taking Control: Decisions and Defining Tasks

Defining what to do is harder. Take the booklist. How many books are students expected to read? How long should a book take? It took me so long to read just a few pages that I felt defeated when I looked ahead. Should I take notes? How many? What would I need them for?

I would sit in the library for a whole day, dipping into one book after another, often with glazed-over eyes. What was my purpose? How would I know when I had achieved it? By comparison I went to lectures gratefully - at least I knew when they started and finished. Although my lecture notes weren't up to much, I could tell myself I had accomplished something, which would bring down my anxiety level.

Much later I discovered I could learn a great deal from close reading of selected sections; that taking notes could sometimes be very satisfying and at other times was not necessary. The trick was to take control; to decide what I wanted to find out - something specific - and then work at it until I had taken in enough to think about for the time being.

Task Division, Targets and Time Allocation

Dividing big jobs into smaller sub-tasks helps to bring work under control, allows you to set targets and check your progress. There is so much pressure to be ambitious - to go for the long dissertation, to read the huge tomes. Yet achievement arises out of quite modest activities undertaken on a small scale. The trouble with the big tasks is that you keep putting them off. Their scope and shape is unclear and we all flee from uncertainty. The more you can define your work as small, discrete, concrete tasks, the more control you have over it.

Organising tasks into the time available can itself be divided into strategy and application. It is useful to think of yourself as 'investing' time. Some tasks require intense concentration and need to be done at a prime time of day, when you are at your best and have time to spare. Others can be fitted in when you are tired, or as 'warm-up' activities at the start of a session. Some, such as essay writing may best be spread over several days. Some need to be done straight away.

There are few reliable guidelines. Essentially you have to keep circling round a self-monitoring loop: plan an approach to a task, try it out, reflect afterwards on your success in achieving what you intended and then revise your strategy.

Once you start to think strategically, you begin to take control of your studies rather than letting them swamp you.

Andrew Northedge. The Open University and author of *The Good Study Guide*, 1991.

9

Source-based Questions

IN PREPARING FOR SOURCE-BASED QUESTIONS students should first be aware of the collections of material available for their subject. On the whole, at A Level, source-based questions are connected with relatively short chronological periods - with Special Subjects or Depth Studies. Nevertheless, the array of relevant documents available can appear daunting, even though what is readily to hand in published form represents only a small proportion of extant material. Source material can never be separated from secondary work; indeed, the line between primary and secondary sources is often very fine. Professional historians use a much wider selection of documents than is available to students, and access to this greater range can therefore be gained at second hand. The work of historians is frequently indispensable in pointing out the limitations of the sources or in reinterpreting the evidence the student will be using. The work of Ralph Griffiths on the evidence (based on pardon lists) for the composition of Cade's rebel host in 1450 provides a striking example. The lists contain the names of a surprisingly large number of gentlemen and others of relatively high social rank. This has led to the conclusion that the rebel army was far from being an irresponsible peasant mob. On closer examination, however, among the names are those of officials against whom the rebels were complaining and those who helped suppress the rebellion. This would lead to the rather different conclusion that not all on the lists were active rebels, but that many individuals had taken advantage of a royal pardon to avoid future prosecution for actions before and during the rebellion, including its suppression. (R. A. Griffiths, *The Reign of King Henry VI*, pp 619-623.)

Preparation may well be easier where examination boards provide collections of prescribed texts, with the assurance that the questions on examination papers will be based on these texts alone. It is even more helpful when there is a close identification of a section of the texts with a section of a paper. Other boards, whilst not prescribing texts, recommend collections of printed documents. Here, the students' task may be a little more difficult but, with the necessary guidance, students can familiarise themselves with the texts which are likely to be put before them. It should be obvious that, for any special subject or depth study, certain documents are central and essential. The English Reformation of the 1530s could hardly be studied without reference to the Act in Restraint of Appeals or the Act of Supremacy. Similarly, the Nuremberg Laws are central to the understanding of Nazi anti-Semitism.

A Hierarchy of Skills

Needless to say, the techniques of handling source material should be tackled regularly in class, as well as by use of and familiarisation with past papers and trial examinations. Although there is a broadly similar policy towards sources on the part of the various examination boards, there are differences of style. Students should be aware of the approaches and question type offered by their particular board. However, virtually all provide a clutch of source material, amounting to a total maximum of about six hundred words, with sub-questions carrying varying weight of marks.

There is a hierarchy of skills in handling source material. At a lower level of difficulty, although vitally important, is comprehension. The passages need to be understood, particularly the key ideas, phrases and words. Language changes, and there are particular problems in the less modern periods.

Comprehending and Comparing

'Dearth', for example, now commonly held to mean 'shortage' was, in the sixteenth century, generally understood to mean 'dearness'. In studying a text such as the Discourse of the

Common Weal, dealing as it does with Tudor inflation and other economic problems, a close understanding of language is essential. Besides being expected to have a general understanding of the passages, students are often required to explain words and phrases or to identify a particular event or personality. Here, although a brief definition may be possible, students should attempt to add further explanation or information relevant to the context in which the word, phrase, event or personality occurs. At the same time, over-lengthy answers should be avoided and, as for other responses, be in proportion to the number of marks allocated for the sub-question.

Within the overall assessment objective of testing the ability of students to use and evaluate source material, questions generally include the requirement to compare two or more sources. Students should ask themselves a series of questions as a way of formulating a response. Do the sources contradict each other? If so, how far and in what ways? Does one add to the impression gained from another? How far do the sources corroborate each other? This last is a vital question since the whole exercise of forming historical judgements is based upon how far one piece of evidence bears out another. One of the great problems of judging the value of the Hossbach Memorandum in the context of Hitler's war and foreign policy has been the lack or paucity of corroboration. On a slightly different but related issue, the student might well come across a document with internal inconsistencies. These should certainly be pointed out as the occasion arises.

Context

Students should be aware of the context of the sources with which they are presented. Sometimes this appreciation is tested directly. On a straightforward level, students should know, without necessarily having to state them, the circumstances surrounding a particular passage, what happened before and how events unfolded afterwards. In a rather higher range, there should be an awareness of how the document relates more widely to the period or subject as a whole. Such an awareness leads to informed judgements about the significance of the material.

All sources have their limitations. These arise out of such

considerations as authorship, bias, misinformation and ignorance, gaps and lack of corroboration. Students need to subject sources to careful and sober evaluation. What are the limitations of a source, how reliable is it, how useful, how significant? An understanding of provenance, or derivation, of a source is essential and the matter of authorship particularly vital. What is known about the writer? How objective or partial is he, does he have an axe to grind? What is the purpose of the document, why was it written, is it deliberately propagandist or perhaps unconsciously partial? Is it a government or official source? The question of whether the author is foreign or native can be important. A very valuable source for the history of late fifteenth-century England is the Italian Dominic Mancini's *Usurpation of Richard III*. It might be argued that as a foreigner he is objective and dispassionate about the controversial matters he is describing. On the other hand, how far did he understand the English political scene and how wide were his sources of information? Foreign ambassadors can be invaluable; their reports are often full and regular. However, they were sometimes in a rather embattled, even isolated, position and their despatches to their masters can reflect this. The letters of the Imperial ambassador, Simon Renard, are an important source for the reign of Mary Tudor. He was close to the centre of events and to the Queen herself, although he is not necessarily a reliable witness. At times he was unduly alarmist about the state of affairs in England, and was critical of the English Council in order to exaggerate his own influence and importance.

Chronological Position and Tone

As well as authorship, students should take particular notice of dating which, where known, is almost always supplied. An obvious consideration is the chronological proximity of an account to the events it describes. A distinction always needs to be made between the date of the event and the date of the account. Eye-witness or near contemporary accounts have their value but can lack perspective and objectivity. The level of involvement can be too great. Careful note should also be taken of the chronological relationship of the sources in a collection to each other. This can be illuminating in dealing with a highly volatile and crowded period such as the French Revolution. The events of the summer of 1789 or of 1793 fall thick and fast in a state of whirling change. A sensitivity to tone and language is essential, and direct questions are sometimes asked about such matters. Is the language extravagant or is it sober and moderate? What words are chosen? Are opponents or other views being condemned rather too vigorously? The language of antagonists in the sixteenth-century European Reformation or of the opponents of Catholicism at the time of the Popish Plot in later seventeenth-century England provide particularly rich examples. The condemnation of the Girondins by their Montagnard rivals during the French Revolution provide excellent examples of bitter political invective. Whilst being aware of tone and language, students should also ask whether an author is attempting to make judgements or is simply describing events.

Sources and the Making of Judgements

Possibly the most difficult skill, and one which is generally highly rewarded, is the ability to bring a whole clutch of documents together and to form an overview. Questions which require this skill generally identify a theme and ask whether or how the sources provide convincing evidence for making judgements or drawing conclusions about it. The approach needs to go beyond paraphrasing along the lines of 'document A says . . . and document B shows . . . whilst document C describes . . .'. Some comprehension skills are required and a certain amount of paraphrasing is probably inevitable, but the theme, or themes, running through the passages, together with related issues and problems, need to be very clearly identified. Then it must be shown how each document handles or bears upon such themes, issues and problems. The approach must be analytical and critical, the value and limitations of the sources need to be assessed and evaluated. Finally, there might be an opportunity for extrapolation. Does the material allow further conclusions to be reached? How far can valid historical judgements be made and what is the scope for personal interpretation?

Neil Hart. Watford Grammar School and A Level Chief Examiner.

10 _____

Revision and Learning

a. The Importance of Attitude

THE METHODS OF STUDYING for exams are as diverse as the individuals who sit them. It is what the individual finds effective and feels happy with, which is of primary importance. After all, it is the student who takes the exam not the teacher and his/her parents. I outline here the method I used and found effective.

Trick or Treat?

After having failed my History 'mock', I started revising for the summer exams quite late, during the summer half-term. By then the exam loomed - an unassailable obstacle to my future happiness. It was probably this which sparked me into an exam frame of mind. It is necessary to see exams not as an adverse and threatening experience, forced upon the unwilling student, but an opportunity and challenge; a test to channel your thoughts, information and ideas to exact questions. The more the student can see the exam as benign and unthreatening the better.

Another lesson to learn is never to underestimate yourself. Sometimes teachers put the emphasis on the danger of thinking you are better than you are but this can be harmful to your confidence in yourself. Your motto should be 'you can do it if you want to' rather than to aim for an average standard.

Method

With regard to method, I make just three points:

- The student needs a comprehensive set of notes on each of the topics on which you think you could answer a question. Organising and going through notes on a topic is itself a way of learning. The notes should be the notes you can understand and to this end underlining dates, highlighting information and creation of sub-headings are useful.

- I found it of central importance to explain my notes to someone else. I discussed my views of individuals, such as Mary Tudor, and the motives behind their actions. It had to be a very dedicated person who was willing to listen to what I said for extended periods of time but requests for explanation and further information encouraged clarity and certainty. To my mind this is extremely valuable because by explaining to someone information and analysis is more readily fixed in the mind.

- Imagination is one of the most important assets a student has. To picture and visualise people from the past, their actions and the events with which they were connected, puts life into the mere words on the page. It also helped me to see perspectives and the arguments over which historians disagree. For example, the Dutch Revolt 1572-1609 may not seem of any contemporary importance but for the rebels, their fight was for freedom from the Spanish and their religious restrictions and tax impositions. Thus many past situations have modern comparisons. If one can only instil the subject with life and bring out its significance then this facilitates exam essay writing because a genuine interest is encouraged. Your own ideas as well as accurate information should be included in essay technique.

To return to my first point, for success in exams one must have motivation - the yearn to learn. If you are not the average genius you need to be willing to sacrifice certain things which will still be there after the exam. Do not be intimidated by the paper, it is there to challenge you not to defeat you.

Howard S.R. Brown gained a Grade C at Advanced Level.

b. Effective Procedure

REVISION FOR A LEVEL is plagued with problems. Each candidate will no doubt have stacks of notes, most of which were written in the previous year and are unrecognisable. Furthermore, each candidate should be aware that some A Level questions are quite specific in what they ask and therefore both a broad and deep knowledge of the subject is required. A further problem is that with two other A Levels also approaching, there are severe time restrictions on the amount of revision that can be done. The best way of tackling these multiple and overlapping problems is to rewrite one's notes in a very concise way, so as to cover all the ground but avoiding information which is irrelevant and wastes one's time.

The Importance of Argument

This essay, while it is applicable to all parts of an A Level History exam, is particularly directed to the Outlines/Aspects/Period Study section (the name varies according to the Examination Board). The A Level student must be able to argue a question cogently. To do this one must have a series of opinions or ideas which can be backed up by evidence. By far the hardest problem is having a valid opinion, which can be made to stand up. The facts and evidence which one uses to justify opinions and themes are relatively easy to obtain and employ.

The first thing one must do is decide which topics are likely to come up and which you plan to answer. Obviously in the space of two years one will cover many topics but on the exam paper you are required to answer only between two to four questions depending on your syllabus and Examination Board; in my case, two English History questions and two European questions. The number of topics it is best to revise is the number of questions to be answered together with a reserve of 50 per cent. If, therefore, the candidate is required to answer four questions on a paper, six topics should be revised. All of these topics must be likely A Level questions because the candidate simply cannot afford to enter an exam and then find out he/she can answer less than the stipulated number of questions. Once the candidate has picked the broad topics which he/she feels reasonably confident with, and expects to have a question on, the examination preparation can begin.

One must have a valid and reasonable opinion on all aspects of a subject before one enters the examination. The candidate will have about one hour in which to write an essay and therefore there is simply not enough time to start formulating new opinions and ideas while in an exam. You must know your views and opinions and apply them to the question asked. A note of warning is required here. You must not go into the exam with an argument, even if it is valid, and apply it no matter what the question asks. You have to analyse the specific question asked. However, the candidate can put himself into a position whereby his arguments will be cogent if he knows his opinions on a subject, and knows that they are reasonable and not over-dogmatic.

One Side of A4

To obtain ideas and views on a subject you must look through your notes. If you can, you should try to get down all the points you will require on one side of a piece of A4. This might well sound too little and you might believe you are oversimplifying a subject, but my experience is that one side of notes is enough. The sort of views and ideas you are trying to obtain are as follows. If one is dealing with a monarch one must ask was he or she a success or a failure? In what respects did he or she succeed or fail: foreign policy, domestic policy, finance, in parliament, economy, law and order? Could he or she have expected to succeed, or were circumstances working against him/her? Obviously, to some extent the candidate can predict the question in relation to each minister/monarch, but it is nevertheless essential that the student has views on all aspects of a reign. It is also essential that the view or opinion is valid and will stand up to the critical eye of the examiner. Do not assume anything in an opinion that you can't back up with event and example and don't be too dogmatic in your argument. Perhaps the best place to search for your views, if you can't remember them, is in the essays which you have completed over the two year course. Hopefully, presuming you are tackling a subject that interests you, you will have your views on that subject readily available. Your essays are useful because it is here that you probably summed up your views on a subject when you actually tackled it. When looking back at past essays you may find your own opinions naive or over simple, so a degree of updating or a different emphasis is sometimes required. Your notes from books and from class taken over the two years should also include some useful opinions, so one shouldn't be short of sources. When you have looked at your essays, examined your notes and, most importantly, thought about your ideas and views, then get them down on one side of a piece of A4.

I have purposely heavily emphasised the need for good, valid and defensible views which lead to concise arguments because I believe this to be the key to A Level success. Anyone can learn a series of facts and turn them out in an exam. This could well show a lot of hard work on the part of the pupil, but it also shows a complete lack of independent thought and ability to use your knowledge in an argumentative way. Turning out facts may earn you a D grade at A Level. However, if you have valid views in a subject which can be employed to tackle any question then a top grade is possible. The joy of having a set of ideas and opinions on a subject is that all A Level questions, despite the fact many may be quite narrow in what they ask, are answerable. Having just a set of facts limits the A Level candidate's scope for improvisation and arguing. This is not to say that facts are irrelevant. Both opinions and facts are required for the high grades at A Level.

The Place for Factual Information

Once candidates have made themselves a sheet of views, then they are in a position to formulate a similar sheet or, perhaps, two, which summarise the main facts and evidence the candidate plans to use. By far the best and most effective type of evidence is primary. In an exam there is not sufficient time to quote historians and put forward vague facts of questionable relevance to the question. Specific references to documents such as parliamentary acts, and the use of definite figures are far more potent weapons to employ in an argument. The best way to obtain one's facts and evidence is by searching through your wad of notes and picking out the relevant points. These are best put under headings such as finance, foreign policy, dynasty etc. Therefore, by the time you have got down five or six facts for each of the headings, you have the evidence which can be used to substantiate the opinions on the first sheet for that topic. If, therefore, you wanted to make the point that, for instance, the Pilgrimage of Grace of 1536 was motivated mainly by Henry VIII's dissolution of the monasteries, then this opinion could be substantiated by reference to the specific demands of the rebel or the Chartist movement was unrealistic and doomed to defeat, then you must know the points of The Charter. Such a view is not too dogmatic and, with supporting evidence, would earn the candidate good marks, assuming it was directly related to the question. Primary evidence is potent because it is unquestionable and useful for a candidate because of the flexible way in which it can be used. It would furthermore be useful to put on your revision sheets general facts about the reign, because these often give a general understanding and coherence to the essay and may help you to answer the exact question set specifically. Such facts as the dates of the start of reigns and some general background to the period in question, and the consequences in the long run of the happenings of the period, are all useful. A knowledge of the periods preceding and succeeding the subject in question are invaluable in providing a wider, broader and more complete argument.

In conclusion, therefore, I can say that my aim is to produce only two to three sides of notes from which we can revise and obtain a high grade at A Level. The harder part of these notes will no doubt be establishing one's own opinions which can be used and made to impress the examiner. Any opinion must then be backed up by evidence to give substance to my point. The facts and figures should be primary and flexible. My final piece of advice is that you should not spend endless nights revising and learning boring dates so that you are tired when entering the exam. An A Level history question must be answered exactly and to the point: there is simply no room for narrative or irrelevance. An analytical argument is produced from a lively, wide-awake mind which knows its opinions and has some factual information to back it up, rather than a dead mind so full of dates and names that there is no room left for improvisation and argument. Just remember that in one hour you are not expected to cover all aspects of a subject. Stick only to what the question asks, and A Levels become far less daunting and instead become an intellectual challenge.

Dominic Haslam gained a Grade A at Advanced Level.

11

Examination Preparation

DURING MY YEARS as an A Level examiner many things about the scripts that I read surprised me. Some scripts were breathtaking in their grasp of historical problems, whereas others made me wonder what had happened to two years of study. However, the most surprising thing was the phenomenon of the 'Centre answer'. This is where all or most of the candidates of one centre (or school) answer the same limited range of questions with almost similar responses - the same structure, the same quotations, the same conclusions. Where this answered the question set, the teacher would no doubt be pleased to see their thoughts reflected so faithfully in the work of their students. Sadly, the 'Centre answer' does not always (or even often) answer the question, and the teacher would be horrified to see that his or her advice to think about and to plan answers had been ignored.

Course-notes which Hinder as well as Help

How can we explain the 'Centre answer'? Surely one of the main reasons must be inefficient examination preparation, and in particular the fact that in the examination itself regurgitation of knowledge comes to overshadow all of the messages that teachers have been sending during the course about the need for historical thinking.

To be more specific, the answer usually lies with the student's file of notes. Consider what you have accumulated already in your course. No doubt there are some notes taken directly from the teacher in class, some notes made from books, some handout sheets, and a few essays. As the stock of notes grows, the problem of how to unlock the information in them grows too. For those who allow this to go on until examinations are imminent, revision will at best salvage something from the accumulated wisdom. At worst, the file of notes will become a real liability. On average, those who learn their notes through will produce a variant on the 'Centre answer' which may well not do them justice.

Despite this depressing scene, revision does tend to be a terminal activity, almost a postscript to the course. Yet, if it is accepted that the quality of examination preparation will significantly influence the final result, common sense dictates that examination preparation should be leading, not following, other activity. Perhaps the first step towards realising this is to drop the word 'revision' in its conventional sense, and to substitute the more specific terms - reworking, review and recall.

Reworking Notes

By reworking we mean structuring, rewriting, tidying, making good, adding points, and improving presentation. Reworking is in many ways the key to success in examination preparation. Look at a sample of class notes. If they were presented by the teacher they should have a sensible structure, but the student will have been so busy writing the notes that hardly any of the content will have been absorbed. The same applies to teachers' handouts, or extracts from books or articles. Often these will have been placed unworked into the file. In both cases reworking provides immediate follow up. This might be the addition of marginal notes, highlighting, underlining, or boiling down into a briefer, more manageable form. This is simply turning them from 'raw' into 'processed' material.

Reworking is even more important where the notes lack a coherent structure. For example, notes made from a teacher's lecture or a discussion may not have the logic of prepared notes. This will be especially true if the discussion digressed, if the talk was hard to follow, or it is last thing on a Friday (or first thing on a Monday). Such notes may require complete restructuring. Gaps will have to be filled, ambiguities clarified, and problems answered by reading or questions in the next lesson. This must be done soon after the notes are made, or it will be impossible to salvage anything from the academic remains of the lesson. Other types of notes will also need reworking as appropriate - for example, notes from texts, or essay notes. All have their use if carefully reworked.

Revision and Recall

Having attended to the immediate problem, the file should not be allowed to lie dormant until the exams loom large. The notes should be regularly reviewed. Review in this sense can simply be reading through the notes, refining, and filling gaps. It is also a necessary process in learning information. Consider the experience of cramming in a frantic two weeks before the examination. Crammed information, learned in sequence, will be repeated in sequence, and more easily forgotten. Long term memory requires repetition or reinforcement, but once this is done it allows greater understanding and flexibility of thought, and closer grasp of detail.

This process of review can therefore be seen as contributing towards the final revision process, that of recall. Ultimately there is a need to know certain information which can be recalled as appropriate. Do not, however, assume that the logical way to generate recall is to revise through your file from one end to the other, one page triggering the next like the cues in a play. If you learn notes in this linear way, it is likely that you will reproduce them in the same way in the exam, whatever the question - and most probably will fall into the trap of writing the narrative style of history which receives so little reward from examiners. Far from this, the order in which you organise learning for recall will have a very significant effect on your examination performance, and it requires very careful planning.

Identifying and Using Key Points

Let us return to the initial reworking of notes. Reworking is all the more important because it will aid later recall and increase the ability to answer the question in a relevant and direct way. The best form of reworking is to identify the small number of key points or ideas which are fundamental aspects of the subject in question. These key points should then be highlighted so that they become the foundation of subsequent revision. The key points may be, for example, causal factors, components, or outcomes of a problem. Each can be thought of as the main point of a paragraph, the detail of which is subsidiary and can be learned at a later stage. In the accompanying diagram a number of key points have been identified within two important subject areas. Having identified key points the examples show how, by applying a variety of questions to that subject area, the key points can be looked at from a number of viewpoints and in a variety of combinations. The effect of this process is to make learning and knowledge flexible, and rooted in clear understanding. This is important because it is a pre-condition for examination answers that the candidate will need to confront the question directly, keep to the point, and avoid narrative. It also allows a variety of styles of revision which will make the process far more interesting and efficient. For example, the sketching out of pattern notes to identify the structure of an answer cannot only provide good reinforcement for revision purposes, but also gives practice in an excellent method of planning essays under examination conditions. This skill can and should be carried into the examination itself.

Reworking to establish key points, then, should be a long-term strategy. There should not be a single page of unworked notes in the file. In parallel with the notes, it may also be considered worthwhile to write revision notes - for example, a set of key points in a jotter or on a card system - as a shorthand revision system which will be of use right up until the moment of the examination. In turn, these will assist in the process of review and recall.

Key Point Dependant Information Detail

What of the mass of fine detail which must be used in support of the key points? This is the body of historical facts and judgements which will make up the bulk of the essay. Key points will provide the structure which will primarily determine the level of mark given by the examiner. Material in support will determine how high within that level the mark will rise. Also, of course, one cannot make bricks without straw; a certain amount of basic knowledge of the period will be taken for granted, and if it is not apparent then essays will not even qualify as historical writing.

For this reason you must get to grips with the fine detail too. If one pursues the idea of key point revision, fine detail should be learned as a dependant of the key point rather than, for example, by whatever came before it in the file. By learning information in 'pockets' like this it makes the whole subject more manageable, flexible and applicable, and less likely to crumble under the pressure of examination.

Revision, then, is far from being an activity which comes at the tail end of the course. If you accept that the notes in your file will play a major part in accumulating and regenerating historical knowledge and understanding, the process of revision must begin at the note-making stage, and must underpin subsequent activity. Certainly this will help you as an individual to think historically and thus to adapt what you know to the specific questions confronting you in the examination. By the way, it will also relieve the examiners from the monotony of the 'Centre answer'.

Scott Harrison. Humanities Adviser, London Borough of Havering.

12

Question and Answer

THE PROCESS OF PREPARING AN EXAMINATION PAPER is long and may take up to two years. Although each examining board works in slightly different ways, these are matter of detail and the boards follow similar procedures.

Question Types: Answer Types

It starts with a chief examiner, a blank piece of paper and a copy of the syllabus. Rough drafts of problems are sketched out, possibly useful quotations are found. Notes of previous examination papers are consulted; a question which proved to be too testing or ambiguous will be avoided. There should be a balance in the types of problems which are set. Some questions will involve comparison, the ability to bring together two or more elements and to assess their significance in relation to each other. ('Compare the contributions of Cavour and Mazzini to the achievement of Italian unification.' 'Which posed the great problem for Elizabeth I, the Catholics or the Puritans?') Answers to such questions should devote approximately equal attention to each aspect. Other questions will be more analytical, requiring answers which focus on particular aspects. ('How far did Henry VII solve his financial problems?' 'How significant was the role of sea-power to the defeat of Nazi Germany in the Second World War?') Although candidates may be able to discuss wider aspects of the problem, the focus should be on the issues which are specifically mentioned in the question. For example, in the question on the Second World War, a candidate might refer to air and land power but will be expected to spend most time discussing naval warfare. Some questions invite candidates to consider more wide-ranging problems as an exercise in making judgements about a lot of material. 'Assess the effects of inflation on sixteenth-century Europe.' 'What was *enlightened* about thought in the eighteenth century?') Other questions might offer a particular point of view for discussion, especially through a quotation. ('The origins of English feudalism are found in the "Norman Conquest". Discuss'. 'How justified is the claim that the origins of the English civil wars are to be found in the reign of James I?') In History, there is no single 'right' or 'wrong' answer and candidates may agree or disagree with the basis of the question; what is important is the quality of the argument which is provided.

Off Limits

There are some sorts of questions which are not acceptable at this level. First, questions should not simply ask candidates to describe what happened. 'What were the most important events of the Thirty Years' War?' would not be a good question because candidates would only have to write a list and would not be guided about the argument which they should use. 'How justified is the claim that the Edict of Restitution was the most important turning point in the Thirty Years' War?' is a much better question. Questions which can only be answered with a knowledge of the most recent research article should be avoided. Whilst up-to-date study is given credit, the rough guide used in drafting questions is that they can be tackled realistically by most candidates who have studied the appropriate sixth-form books on the subject. But it does require reading beyond the standard outline textbooks for anything above the lowest grades.

All examining boards now set questions on documents and these are different in format from the essay questions; the qualities which they test are also different. These document questions are usually sub-divided into parts and the boards often provide an indication of the marks as a guide to the length of time to be devoted to each part. The short questions which are given 1 or 2 marks need to be answered exactly as well as briefly. Other questions must be worded very clearly to make it apparent how they are to be tackled, whether the documents are to be analysed or compared, or how far the answers should be confined to the printed documents and how far outside references are needed. In these questions, the instructions such as 'analyse' or 'compare' or 'using only these documents' should be followed precisely.

Gradually, the jig-saw is put together and the first draft is ready. A moderator will then look at the paper. He is an independent person, not an examiner, who is given a special responsibility by a board for ensuring that papers are fair. He will assess whether the questions reflect a balanced view of the syllabus or whether major areas are omitted. This does not mean, for example, that there will always be a question on Luther or Gladstone but there should be something on the Reformation or liberalism or the Irish problem if these are significant parts of the syllabus. The wording of questions must be absolutely clear; there must be no hidden clues or implications which are not immediately evident to candidates as they read the question papers in the tense atmosphere of an examination room. The questions must be possible for the less able candidates who are hoping for an E grade and they must also offer scope to the potential A grade students. They should not reflect too closely questions which have been set in very recent examinations but that does not mean that similar questions cannot be set again if they offer a fair test. For example, a question on Louis XIV's responsibility for the wars after 1689 might be followed in the next year by one on the aims of his foreign policy. The papers should be neither more nor less difficult than previous papers and should compare well with papers set by other boards so that candidates face a similar level of examination whichever syllabus and board they prepare for.

It may take several drafts before the chief examiner and moderator are satisfied. The next stage involves a meeting, perhaps more than one meeting, at which a cross-section of teachers, other experienced people and staff from the examining board are present. The paper is again looked at in detail, questions are cut, amended, polished and finally agreed. So, two years is not too long a time to prepare and mark a paper.

Russell Williams. Cheltenham and Gloucester College.

Seven Don'ts for Answer Writers by Russell Williams

• <u>Don't be irrelevant.</u> Irrelevance is probably the most common reason why candidates in History examinations gain disappointing results. You must remember that you are answering a question set by somebody else. The purpose is to discover if you can select from the material which you have learned the arguments and factual knowledge which are appropriate to deal with this question. Hundreds of questions can be set on the causes of the Reformation or on Gladstonian liberalism and the test is whether you can discuss effectively this year's question, not whether you have a general knowledge of the topics. Although you may have worked hard to prepare for the examination, do not simply write out a prepared answer. Think about what this year's question demands.

• <u>Don't be disorganised.</u> Answers should be presented in a straightforward and clear manner. There is insufficient time in an examination to write out long plans but it is useful to jot down the main points and then put them into order. Discuss first the most important issues and spend more time on them. By the end of your answer, you should be dealing with less important issues which can be covered quite briefly.

• <u>Don't write long introductions.</u> A lot of candidates worry unnecessarily about introductions. As a general rule, it is better to begin discussing the question immediately. There is no need to explain the general background to problems and a well-focused discussion is more effective. There is sometimes a temptation in popular topics to try to mention many side issues at the beginning. But, for example, if a question is on the foreign policy of Napoleon I, candidates will receive little credit if they write several paragraphs on his domestic policies at the beginning.

• <u>Don't write general descriptions.</u> At A Level, questions do not ask *what* happened and candidates should avoid writing only narratives of events. Questions tend to ask about reasons ('Why did Peter the Great attempt to westernise Russia?'). They may be concerned with consequences ('Explain the effects of the First World War on British society in the 1920s'). They may ask candidates to compare people or factors ('Compare the dangers to the Elizabethan religious settlement presented by the Catholics and Puritans'). Look for key words in questions, such as 'Explain', 'To what extent?' and 'Analyse' and use them to frame your answers.

- <u>Don't write waffle.</u> This is when candidates write in very general terms, not mentioning the elements of the question and providing few supporting facts. The wording of the question should direct you to the issues to be discussed. A Level questions are clear and candidates should not fear traps or hidden clues but the questions themselves state issues which must be discussed. A question on the reasons why Hitler gained power in Germany should not be an opportunity to describe the general course of German history from the rule of Bismarck. Instead examiners are looking for a concentrated explanation of the rise of Hitler: What did it depend on? What was the role of the army and other political parties? How influential was the personal influence of Hitler? Why did the opposition prove ineffective? Such points as these should be supported by relevant factual knowledge. When did Hitler come to power? Who were the main leaders of the army and of the other political parties?
- <u>Don't quote excessively.</u> Examiners will give credit for relevant and appropriate quotations or references to historians but it is better to use a few quotations or references to historians and then to discuss them than to sprinkle essays with quotations in an unselective way. Answers often show that candidates have not read or understood the historians who are mentioned and cannot use the quotations to advance their arguments. Credit is given when candidates show by brief comments that they understand the significance of what historians have written. Avoid quotations which have become clichés; for example, it is rarely useful to describe James I as 'the wisest fool in Christendom'.
- <u>Don't run out of time.</u> The questions are designed so that candidates can answer them adequately in the available time. Examiners do not expect long and detailed answers. It is a mistake to spend too long on a question about which you know a lot and then run out of time by the end of the examination. Long answers might indeed earn a few extra marks but the marks lost by a later incomplete or note-form answer will usually be more and you will be penalising yourself. Unnecessarily long answers usually contain an excessive amount of factual material. Remember that the examiner is looking primarily at the quality of the argument, supported by appropriate factual material. An answer which has a direct argument and which includes appropriate factual knowledge will often be worth more marks than a long and detailed essay which contains an unclear argument.

13

The Marking of Scripts

IT MAY TAKE SEVERAL DRAFTS before the chief examiner and moderator are satisfied with a question paper. The next stage involves a meeting, perhaps more than one meeting, at which a cross-section of teachers, other experienced people and staff from the examining board are present. The paper is again looked at in detail, questions are cut, amended, polished and finally agreed.

The exam day comes and all that the candidates have to do is to sit in a hall and write. Two and a half or three hours later (dependent on the Examination Board), it is all over. But the examiners' tasks are just beginning. Instructions on how the marking should be done arrive through the letter-box and have to be noted. Somewhere in the process of preparing the paper, the chief examiner will have prepared a mark-scheme giving guidance to examiners on how the answers should be marked. A meeting is held, attended by all examiners, when the question paper and the mark-scheme are discussed, because it is obviously important that all examiners mark to the same standards. For example, if a question is on Lenin's career and an answer does not begin until after the Russian Revolution, what maximum marks might be allowed?

Positive Marking

The examiners then begin their marking. In spite of what candidates fear, the examiners do not start by looking for the errors, omissions and other faults in a script. These do count, of course, but the first task is to look for the positive aspects of an answer. What is relevant? What is the candidate trying to say? Is the supporting factual evidence appropriate? Is the argument easy to understand? When the positive points have been assessed, the examiners then look for the shortcomings. Most important, we must remember the sort of candidate who is usually being assessed: about eighteen years of age, having studied the syllabus for two years along with other subjects, hardworking(!) and almost always making a serious effort to grapple seriously with the problems which are set in the examination paper. This is as true of most students who are aiming for an E grade as of the students who hope for an A. Examiners do not set out to pass or fail a certain proportion of candidates. The results depend on the quality of work which is seen.

Even Standards

Samples of scripts are exchanged regularly between the examiners, so that senior examiners can ensure that candidates are being marked to the same standard. This avoids the possibility of individual examiners taking too tough, or too easy, a line with certain questions. It also gives senior examiners a feel for the way in which candidates as a whole are tackling the paper. Perhaps some questions are posing unexpected difficulties.

When the marking is complete, other procedures take place to ensure that all the examiners have marked to the same standard. If the overall results of one examiner's marking seem to be tougher or more lenient than others, the marks may be reviewed and that examiner can be scaled to bring him into line with others. The results of different papers are compared because candidates' results should not be affected by the particular papers which they have sat. If necessary, the results of an entire paper can be scaled.

Setting Grade Boundaries

An important decision still has to be made about marks and grades. Perhaps the vital decision for most candidates is the mark needed for a bare pass at Grade E. Although it is expected at the beginning that 40 will be the pass mark in each paper, this may be changed marginally, dependent on the views of a lot of people who have been involved in the examining process. For example, in spite of all the safeguards when the paper was set, it might be thought that it was more difficult than usual. In this case, the pass mark might be changed slightly to about 39. Similar decisions also have to be made about the marks needed for other grades.

Double Checking

There are still other checks which have to be made. Unexpected discrepancies between a candidate's pair of scripts - a high mark on one script and a low mark on another - will result in a review of both scripts. Some borderline scripts, where the results are just under a grade, may be read again. Some examining boards ask centres to send in estimates of their results and if some candidates have done far differently than expected their scripts may be checked. Centres' results can be compared with those of previous years because, on the whole, their results can be expected to be about the same; significant differences in any one year can justify a check of scripts.

Two years is not too long a time to prepare and mark a paper. The daunting thought is that whilst sixth-formers are beginning their studies, examiners are already beginning to think about the papers they will sit.

Russell Williams. Cheltenham and Gloucester College and Chairman of the Award, Cambridge Local Examinations Syndicate.

14

ACE Essay Grades:

Grade Differentiation

ADVANCED LEVEL EXAMINERS do not have specific grades in mind when they mark essays. Grading is done by Chief Examiners at the end of the process when a candidate's whole 'profile' can be judged. Also, since essay questions allow for a wide variety of valid answering strategies, it can never be possible to identify all the characteristics which every essay gaining marks which equate with a given grade will have. However, some broad generalisations can be made about history essays written under examination conditions. It may therefore be useful to summarise the qualities frequently found in essays of different quality. As a rough guide, and certainly not to be taken as definitive indicators, these characteristics are related to grades.

In order to make the best use of what follows, it is worth knowing that most A Level history essays are a mixture of 'narrative' (providing basic information about a period or topic usually in chronological form) and 'analysis' (involving discussion, debate, argument relevant to the question asked). For higher marks, examiners will want to see analytical skills predominating over 'accumulative' or fact-bound ones.

Grade A

Most essays of this quality will have a good basic grasp of the factual content relating to the topic and will use it with discrimination and selectivity. These essays will usually have been written by candidates who know that they have more knowledge about the topic than they can possibly use in the 45 minutes or one hour available to them. Thus the evidence which appears in the essay will have been appropriately selected. The criteria for selection will relate to the precise wording of the question. These essays will relate precisely to the question asked. The question's focus will have clearly been understood. If, for example, the question required discussion of 'Why, and to what extent' some phenomenon occurred, the A-grade essay will pay attention to both parts. The emphasis in the answers will be on argument, the candidate having recognised that examiners want to see appropriately supported *judgement* or *debate*. A-grade essays will not be 'model answers'. Roughly 10 per cent of candidates obtain grade A and few of them are budding Gibbons or Macaulays. They will, however, have the right balance between evidence and argument and they will pay precise attention to the wording of the question as they develop their arguments. Don't forget, also, that the great majority of A-grade essays are pretty well written. History is in significant part a literary discipline and the best candidates are clearly aware of this as they prepare their work. Never ignore the vital skill of communication. It is a very important discriminator.

Grade C

In the middle ranges, obviously, advanced historical skills are less well developed. Some essays in this category are grounded in a very secure knowledge of the topic and will include some narrative passages. They will obtain marks which equate with a C because they also have significant passages of analysis, certainly more than would be found merely in an introduction and conclusion. An increasing number of 'C' essays these days have little or no narrative, concentrating on direct responses to the question asked. However, the analysis may be partial; some elements in the question may be very lightly treated so that the whole answer is 'unbalanced' (to use examiner jargon). Or the response may contain confused passages, or sentences which do not clearly relate to what has gone before. Some otherwise good answers 'fall back' because the candidate has not demonstrated sufficiently precise knowledge of the topic to convince that they can sustain and substantiate argumentative points. Examiners make clear distinctions between historical argument and analysis (which is supported and sustained) and 'assertion' (which is not). All C-grade essays will contain good things. The mixture between the good and the not so good, however, varies widely.

Grade E

This is the minimum passing grade and examiners are looking for sufficient evidence of historical competence in order to award it. It follows that they *are* looking for positive virtues and will not award marks in this range on sympathy or in recognition of an adequate memory or an ability to write fast. Most E-grade answers show sufficient knowledge of the topic to indicate that its essentials have been understood. An accurate narrative answer with an introduction and conclusion which genuinely addresses the issue in the question will almost always be worth a minimum pass. Depending on the quality of the information, and the skill with which it is deployed, some narratives will deserve more than the minimum passing marks. Some very worthy candidates in this range are held back from higher award by poor literary skills. They cannot express themselves confidently or with cogency. They cannot therefore convince the examiner of how much they *understand* about the topic. The more difficult essay to judge in this borderline range is the one (increasingly common) which appreciates what skills are required and has a basic grasp of at least some of the essentials but which is lightweight overall. A large number of such essays are based on insufficient reading. Here examiners are looking for sufficient evidence of understanding which goes beyond vague assertion. Examiners are always more impressed by *precise* reference to evidence material than by generalised references or hopeful statements which yearn for a fact or two in support. At this level, examiners are not looking for sustained and well-judged balances between evidence and argument but they do demand some precision, mostly relevant references and indications in the essay that at least part of the point of the question has been grasped.

Professor Eric Evans. University of Lancaster and A Level Chief Examiner.

15

The Individual Study

The High Grade Response

MANY, PERHAPS MOST, candidates can expect to raise their overall grades by their performance in the Individual Study. Whilst there are many very competent pieces of work, however, the highest grades, A and B, are reserved for those Studies which demonstrate a sharp understanding of historical problems and the ability to communicate ideas and arguments in a clear, coherent fashion.

High quality Studies are, needless to say, a direct reflection of the quality of preparation. Very close attention should be given not only to the regulations for the examination but also to the notes provided for the guidance of candidates by the examination board. The choice and exact wording of the title is crucial. Wide and very generalised subjects rarely result in the highest grades. Apart from anything else, very broad subjects cannot be satisfactorily investigated in the limited number of words available. Instead the title should be sharply focused and problem-centred, and it is a good idea to frame it as a question. In the examiner's mind a sharp title sets the agenda for the Study which follows.

Analysis, Insight, Argument and Judgement

The time allocated to research should be generous. It is important to consult a wide range of authorities and there must be adequate time for ideas to mature and take shape. Examiners can almost invariably tell whether the material has been processed through a candidate's mind. They are not impressed by hastily assembled work put together by 'scissors and paste' methods. Neither are they inclined to reward over-reliance on a small handful of books which borders on plagiarism. Again, work which consists of nothing beyond solid narrative with no evidence of thought, analysis or argument cannot get beyond the lower grades.

It may seem to be rather elementary advice, but so many candidates fail to appreciate that a high standard of presentation is essential. The Study is not affected by the pressures of a timed examination. This is one reason why so many candidates can lift their overall grade by means of the Study. The penalty of a more spacious time allocation, however, is that examiners give no quarter when grammar, punctuation, syntax and spelling are sloppy. Word processors can often betray candidates into avoidable errors. All work, however produced, must be checked and corrected as necessary. As to style, the very best pieces of work are invariably clear and fluent and the examiners pencil flows benevolently over them.

There is no automatic credit for choosing unusual subjects but the candidate who has chosen a field away from the already well-trodden paths, by the very exercise of initiative in choosing, often produces a Study which has outstanding qualities across the board.

It is not absolutely essential to make use of primary source material. For some subjects such material is not readily available. Nevertheless, for a large number of subjects, with a reasonable amount of effort, published source material can be obtained. For studies in local history, of course, a whole range of opportunities presents itself. Needless to say, if candidates do not make use of source material, the evaluation and interpretation of which is one of the assessment objectives for all Advanced Level courses, their Studies will need to be exceptionally strong in almost all other respects in order to gain one of the higher grades.

Clarity, Focus and Understanding

It is a rare Study which has no narrative dimension. Some narrative is inevitable and considerable credit can be gained for the clarity, focus and understanding with which it is presented. It is the Study which fails to go beyond narrative or is overburdened with it which falls down. The higher grades can be gained only by those candidates who demonstrate real insights into the material, identify and analyse themes and problems and develop a coherent argument. Above all, the A-grade candidate is able to form personal judgements based on a close understanding of the material and a critical evaluation of the evidence.

Finally, it is difficult to quantify the degree of enthusiasm and commitment conveyed by a Study. Nevertheless, these rather intangible qualities do shine through. The choice of title is one sign as is the presentation. However, the real proof, which examiners certainly pick up, lies in the combination of critical interpretation, informed personal judgement and a clear sense of involvement.

Neil Hart. Watford Grammar School and A Level Chief Examiner.

The Personal Study: Steps to Success

The Self-study Programme which makes the Personal Study the most rewarding and highly-graded work for the Advanced Level Student.

- Step 1   Think of three or four topics on which you would like to write. Investigate in libraries to which you have access and journals (such as *History Review*) whether there are books for these topics. Look at the bibliographies of books you find to see if further books are recommended (and the date of their publication - books published many years ago may be unobtainable).

- Step 2   Choose one topic (for which there is adequate information) and submit the title and booklist to the Examination Board as instructed. Await acceptance by the Board.

- Step 3   Follow up references and bibliographies on your chosen topic, in the books and journals to which you have access, for further sources. Assess the usefulness and value to you and your topic of the books/sources mentioned. Critical bibliographies are especially helpful with this.

- Step 4   Read a concise general account of your topic to gain a survey/overview of the subject.

- Step 5   Consider the survey/overview and decide which are the important questions which need to be answered on your topic. You should have between 7 and 20 questions.

This is the key stage of your Individual/Personal Study work.
Be sure that you ask important questions and that they are not
trivial/superficial. Write a list of your questions: *this list will be
central to your work programme hereafter.*

- Step 6 Select one or two of your questions. They need not be
the first questions on your list and they need not be the earliest
chronologically. Your selection may be influenced by the
information (books/articles) you have in your possession at the
time.

Survey the sources that relate to the one or two questions you
have chosen. Choose one or two to be the primary source of
information, because of their suitability and power of analysis,
for that question.

Read only those parts/pages of the chosen sources that help
you toward an answer to your question. Make *brief* notes. You
should not need to make extensive notes (especially if you have
constant access to the source). Record the author, title of
book/journal article, date of publication and page references
for every source from which you make notes.

Having researched the answer to the question record in good,
clear English your conclusion/answer. Write every other line
because this will be part of the first draft of your Study.

- Step 7 Repeat Step 6 for your other questions. Start the
answer to a new question on a new sheet of paper.

- Step 8 (to be followed *during Steps 6 and 7*) Keep alert for
further sources (see Step 3) which could help you answer your
questions well. *Be ready to change your questions* (Step 5) - by
addition, deletion or modification - as you gain more
understanding of your topic.

- Step 9 Order your answers from Steps 6 and 7 in a way that
provides the most effective analysis of your topic. This is the
first draft of your Individual/Personal Study.

- Step 10 Read, revise and polish, both content and English
style, your first draft. Allow at least 10 days for this step. Write
your introduction when this is finished. Then write a well
presented final draft and deliver it to your teacher on time.

Gilbert Pleuger.

16

Study and Knowledge

HAVE YOU READ a book which transformed your view about a subject? Many people have. I did. I was at college and I borrowed from the library a book by C.A. Mace called *The Psychology of Study* (first edition 1932). It led me to recognise that I had wasted many hours during my A Level years. Study, I began to recognise, was more than something students did - it should be thought about. Study was an activity which a student could undertake efficiently or inefficiently. That book by C.A. Mace began my continuing interest in study skills.

Then last summer I was at Hatfield in Hertfordshire. I had taken photographs of the Cecils' Hertfordshire seat and while I sat in the sun at the café in the former stableyard I glanced at a book I had bought. Written by Graham Gibbs, it summarised research on how students learn.[1] This is not a book about memory and memorisation techniques but about how students may better understand the nature of the learning task - and the learning task varies in accordance with the subject. To learn for an historian is not the same as to learn for a physicist. As happened years before with the book by C.A. Mace, my view of the study task was transformed. I would never see study skills in the same way.

Study Skills and Attitudes to Knowledge of the Past

The implications of Graham Gibbs's book is that study skills *can be* helpful toward success but are not, by themselves, guarantors to success.

Students need to experiment with techniques of study, reading, note making, writing essays . . . the skills that have been mentioned in the previous pages, and to assess which techniques are effective *for them*. Active reflection is required to consider what they want to do in their study, how to undertake it and an assessment of the extent to which the methods used further success.

Students, to achieve well, need to take responsibility for the way they study and not rely on their teachers. If they rely on their teachers they remain merely passive recipients of information, ideas and advice. Even more, they need to relate study techniques to a wider appreciation of how they see the study of history and how they see history.

More fundamental than study skills is the use to which study skills are put. The use will reflect the student's approach to the subject, to history. The approach more than the study method will influence the outcome of study.

Picturing the Past

Does the student see study as the acquisition of information (which can be achieved by rote learning) or as an inquiry into how and why the past was the way it was and what historians have thought about it?

When the study of history is seen in the wider context of the real past (and not a 'book' past, not just 'facts' in a book or from a lecture) students will relate information from their study about history by creating a 'dialogue' between their information and a wider context which will include:

- People, their nature and needs - both in the present and the past - human nature is the constant in history.
- The social, economic and political background to the topic studied.
- The ways of operation of society and/or politics, local, national and international, at the time.
- The relationship of individuals and institutions at the time: how individuals and groups interacted with institutions.
- The ideas of the time, and the responses of individuals and/or groups to the ideas.

With this, a more vital appreciation of the past, students will wish to compare their views about the past with the views of others, whether in books or tutorials . . . and the student will have some recognition that history is that part of the past that we, in the present, can understand and recreate: it is that part of a jigsaw picture that is assembled when many parts of the jigsaw are missing. History books represent a dialogue between the present (the work of the historian) and the past. The latitude available in the recreation of the past will lead to a variations among historians in their understanding and the debate between historians generated by this variation of understanding is a valuable contribution to students' appreciation of the past and to their own understanding.

Note

1 Graham Gibbs, *Teaching Students to Learn. A Student-Centred Approach*, Open University Press, 1981.

Gilbert Pleuger.

Core Concepts,
Terms and
Ideologies

oncepts

liberalismsocialismliberalismsocia-
lismliberalismsocialismliberalism-
socialismliberalismsocialismliibera-
lismsocialismliberalismsocialismli-
beralismsociaalismliberalismmsocia-
lismliberalismsocialismliberalismso-
cialismliberalismssocialismli-
beralismsocialismliberaalismsocia-
lismliberalismsociallismliberalismso-
cialismliberalismsocialismliberalism-
socialismliberaliismsocialismliber-
lismsocialismliberalismsocialismli-
beraalismsocialismliberalismsocial-
lismliberalismsocialismliberalisms-

ideology

17 Sovereignty

Among theories seeking to justify political power, sovereignty is particularly the concept which legitimates the existence of a final and absolute authority within the political society by reconciling the conflicting instinctive beliefs of the ruler and the ruled about the source of power.

From Populist to Absolutist Justification

In pre-state or stateless communities the immediate source of power is instinctively assumed to lie in the Community itself. Their theories about rulership, such as they are, are populist. Nor is it solely for this reason that the power of the rulership, such as it is, is not seen to be final and absolute. The Rights of the Community themselves are enshrined in custom or law derived from a higher external source; the ultimate source of authority lies in Nature or with the gods. These attitudes are so tenacious that such communities tend to sub-divide rather than accept the growth of population, the increase of territory or the greater complexity of affairs that undermines the viability of their lineage systems and calls for the distinctive form of rule associated with the State. In the cities of classical Greece, the most sophisticated of stateless societies, the propensity to avoid these developments by founding new cities went hand in hand with an inveterate distrust of monarchy.

In the circumstances in which the State emerged, it, too, almost invariably subscribed to the notion that its authority was limited by a higher power. But it derived its right to rule directly from that power; the Ruler was the agent on earth of the gods. Its theory about rule was theocratic and, in relation to the Community, it was instinctively absolutist.

The Roman Illusion

The rise of the Emperorship in Rome in the first century AD, an outstanding exception to this generalisation, provided an early, and an isolated, illustration of the process by which the concept of sovereignty encapsulates the need for compromise between populist and absolutest justifications of ultimate authority by asserting the constitutional legitimation of absolute power. Alone among the cities of the ancient world, the Roman republic became an extensive empire. Alone among the primitive states of that world, the Roman state originated in the principate, the office of chief citizen or first magistrate of the Roman people, and evolved into an Emperorship which governed with absolute power. But the manner in which the Emperor had acquired his power was reflected in the legal doctrine that it had its origin in the will of the Community. 'What has pleased the Prince has the force of law inasmuch as . . . the People transfers to him and into his hands all its own Right and power.'

In the conditions which followed this first formulation of sovereignty, the concept could make no headway against the alternative thesis that the Ruler derived his power from the gods. In Rome, as in Byzantium, the Emperorship remained in theory elective, but it degenerated into a theocracy in which the absolutism of the ruler was tempered only by assassination and deposition. Islam, failing to develop a state, established only a ritual theocracy over a multiplicity of tribes and stateless communities which it did not govern. In Europe the Pope and the Emperor failed to establish more than a ritual ascendancy over Christendom - failed to resuscitate the Roman Empire in the West - from the time when its separate societies underwent rule by states during the sixth century. It was in those societies that sovereignty would eventually be re-formulated, but insuperable obstacles barred the way to its emergence throughout the Middle Ages. With the profound desecularisation of thought which accompanied the rise of Christendom, an external Divine Law both sanctified the customary law of the Community and accentuated the priestly character of the Ruler as the agent of God. The Ruler was also the elect of the Community; but in this capacity he undertook to observe the higher law which protected the Rights of the Community against his intrusion. And if this outlook required king and community to inhabit separate spheres, the decentralised condition of the society ensured that they remained distinct.

core concepts, terms and ideologies

Conflicting Authorities in Post-Medieval Europe and the Thomist Compromise

By the thirteenth century the slow accretion of government power, the quickening of activity in the community and the recovery of the writings of Greece and Rome had undermined the medieval structure of thought. It was recognised that society needed an enacted positive law that was different from the Divine Law, and some authority that was superior to at least the positive law. But far from leading to the formulation of the concept of sovereignty the outcome of this advance was a prolonged bedlam of conflicting qualified views about the source and extent of political power within an actual confusion of overlapping authorities. Within the kingdom some argued that the superior authority could only be the Ruler, but accepted that his freedom was limited to his executive powers, while others insisted that supremacy resided in the People, which possessed in its Estates a continuous legislative control over even his executive acts. Within Christendom the recovery of Roman law accentuated disputes as to how far the Kingdoms were subject to which of the universal authorities, Pope or Emperor. Nor is that all. The dominant ideology of the thirteenth, fourteenth and fifteenth centuries was the synthesis of the Christian cosmology with Aristotelianism in which Aquinas and the Humanists, rejecting the need for an ultimate, earthly authority, reconciled the *de jure* universality of papal imperial power with the *de facto* existence of the regional kingdoms and insisted that, within each semi-autonomous kingdom, government by the Ruler was compatible with the fact that magnates and people remained supreme in their own estates. The Ruler was supreme in some contingencies and the Community in others, and normally the two would work in harmony.

The Issue Restated during the Renaissance and Reformation

By the sixteenth century, this synthesis was being shattered by the intellectual changes which had produced the Renaissance and the Reformation, and the more rapid centralisation of government and the increasing articulation of the Community were combining with those changes to drive some of the European kingdoms into civil and religious war. And it was in these circumstances that Bodin in 1576 propounded the concept of sovereignty as the sole means of escape from irreconcilable conflict between the Ruler, who had now rejected the elective element in his accession by claiming an hereditary Divine Right to rule, and the Community, which was taking its right to resistance to the lengths of justifying tyrannicide.

Theories of Sovereignty: Bodin, Hobbes and Rousseau

Bodin argued that in a body politic consisting of Ruler and Ruled, the Ruler must be sovereign in the sense that he was above the positive law and exercised this prerogative without the subject's consent, but that his power was not rightly exercised (though it might not be resisted) if he ignored the moral dictates of the divine (natural) law and the fundamental (customary) rights of the Ruled. Subsequent advocates of sovereignty argued that, by insisting both on the logical necessity of sovereign power and on the proper limits to it, he formulated the doctrine only to obscure it at once. Hobbes in *Leviathan* (1651) dismissed the ancient belief in a contract between the People and the Ruler by extinguishing altogether the personality of the People in favour of the equal rightlessness of individuals before the Ruler who was their own creation and whose will was the will of every subject. For Hobbes's opponents sovereignty remained with the People by virtue either of a contract with the Ruler or of an initial contract between individuals which was prior to all political organisation and made their rights inalienable; and on the strength of this initial contract Rousseau in *The Social Contract* (1762) took over every ingredient in Hobbes's argument and made it yield, not the absolutist sovereignty of the rulership, but the populist sovereignty of the Community. But these extreme statements of the concept only prolonged the conflicts which it was its function to heal.

Core concepts, terms and ideologies

Hobbes might advance the novel view that the personality of a body politic composed of Ruler and Ruled was the wielder of sovereign power, and might regard it as a matter of choice or circumstance whether the Ruler was one physical person or a few or many, but in view of the undeveloped character of the organs and procedures of government in his day, the Ruler could only be the old Prince made absolute. Rousseau might demote government to be a commission from the sovereign People, which was automatically suspended when the People assembled; but he discarded the organs and procedures of government, without which no body politic has been able to function since the State succeeded to the tribe and the city, in favour of the general will, which can practically find expression only in the populist tyranny of the dictator or the crowd.

The Modern Compromise: Executive Power, Rules of Execution and Institutions which Represent the Community

It is by avoiding these extremes, on the other hand, that modern formulations of the concept have put controversy to rest. They all seek to replace the old dualism of Ruler and People by a correlation of their rights and needs in a notional body politic which the executive state and the community of citizens have combined to create, which is sovereign over both, and which embodies its sovereignty in such fashion as allows the State the power of decision provided it abides by rules - the Crown-in-Parliament, the Constitution, a fundamental law - which meet the needs and retain the consent of the community.

Sir Harry Hinsley. St John's College, Cambridge.

18 Power, Society and Economy

The theme of power runs like a six-lane motorway through the delicate landscape of examination syllabuses for most Advanced Level and younger undergraduate students.

Power is Influence

Influence is the most helpful synonym for power. Everyone exercises power, whether it is the toddler whose cry evokes the response of the mother, the young person in love who is so willing to please or the pensioner who commands the care of others. Many would describe these exercises of power, or influence, at the inter-personal level as part of the give-and-take of a relationship but they do, nevertheless, embody the central characteristic of power - that is, influence on the actions and behaviour of others. Power can be discerned in any area of activity. In sport, a football manager will have power, partly *ex officio,* by right of his office as manager and consequent right to make team arrangements and buy and sell players, but he will also have influence over the players because of the person he is, his standing as a manager and (maybe) as a former player, and his influence with the players will be seen by their loyalty, commitment and effort as they strive to win matches. The exercise of power by an individual *ex officio* may be called the formal exercise of power. Power, as influence on the actions of others, which is not *ex officio* may be called the informal exercise of power. The first examples, the baby, the young lovers and the old age pensioner are, of course, examples of the informal exercise of power.

In the world of the arts, entertainment and fashion notable persons will exercise power. Their ideas and actions, sometimes encapsulated as style, influence the ideas and actions, the cultural behaviour, of others. Two better-known examples are Picasso, whose styles of painting influenced many artists of his generation and the Rolling Stones who helped establish the distinctive teenage culture of the 60s.

Exercises of Power

There is a spectrum of ways in which power is expressed. Five points on the spectrum are taken to illustrate this. Near one end of the spectrum power, that is influence over the behaviour of others, follows from those who are seen as heroes or idols because those who admire or adore them

Core concepts, terms and ideologies

imitate their behaviour. In a less extreme instance, a person may be respected, if not adored, and because of this respect others will more willingly accept requests or orders from that person. More central to the range of types of power exercise, power may be expressed as a consequence of reasoning in discussion, debate or argument. For example, a workshop manager discusses the company's trading position with the employees and they agree to change their work arrangements. If persuasion by discussion is ineffective, a person who wants to influence a person's behaviour may need to provide incentives or bribes or make threats. The footballer may agree reluctantly to team tactics rather than be dropped from the team, the student delivers the work assignment only three days late to avoid the threatened penalty of reduced marks, the workers increase output in exchange for a higher rate of pay and the gangster pays up as ordered by the godfather when the safety of his wife and child are threatened. There are times when neither reasoning nor threats achieve the wanted influence over others and their behaviour. In these circumstances behaviour will be influenced only after the use of physical force. After the Argentinian occupation of the Falklands and the ineffectiveness of diplomatic discussion and threats of military action - that is, attempts to *persuade* the Argentinians to leave, the armed forces physically removed Argentinian soldiers from the Falkland Islands. A joy-rider who re-offends time and time again is eventually barred from access to cars by being locked in prison.

A period of political revolution is a particularly interesting time for the study of the exercise of power. The exercise of power by the would-be revolutionaries will be discerned before the government is changed as they seek to win the support of the people and undermine the loyalty to the government. This may be depicted as an attempt to win the minds of the populace. On the day or days of the revolution, force is used to physically remove the incumbent government: power is exercised (with the help of automatic weapons, tanks, artillery . . .) and ministers are arrested or killed. When the old government is removed the new government will make decisions and issue commands and seek to enforce obedience. If obedience is achieved by willing acceptance

without the use of physical constraint, because the minds of
the populace is won to an acquience of the new government
either by propaganda and argument or else by threats or fear,
the security of the new government will be greater. When the
new government has changed its strength from power into
authority its foundation will be more firm for, as Rousseau
wrote in *The Social Contract*, (1762) 'The strongest is never
strong enough to be always master, unless he transforms
strength into right, and obedience into duty'.

Political Power

Politics and political activity describes the activity of either all
of society (such as the free men in the Greek city states) or, in
larger societies, some members of it and their work of making
decisions and implementing decisions when made for the
protection, ordering and well-being of that society and its
members. In modern states these activities at the national
level are focused upon organisations, such as parties, and
institutions, such as parliaments, cabinets, civil services . . . In
the less complicated early-modern states the comparable
components were factions, monarchs and their courts, then
councils, estates, exchequers and so on. Taken together, the
procedures and institutions constitute the government. Common to both early-modern and modern government are ways
to make decisions for the populace and administer and
enforce these decisions. During the twentieth century, furthered by the economic dynamic and two world wars, the
busyness of government has increased and decisions, enacted
as laws, now regulate almost every area of life.

    If the last paragraph is taken as a summary of politics,
political power will be seen to describe activity which has any
bearing on the making or the implementing of decisions - for
the protection, ordering or well-being of society. Interest
groups have exactly that aim. Better known interest groups
include the CBI and the TUC but organisations such as the
RSPB and Oxfam have political power as does the press. Even
a college seminar in which the opinions of voters is influenced is an example of power, albeit in a minimal way. Within
the structure of political institutions, political activity may be

core concepts, terms and ideologies

depicted as moving from the base of the political structure toward the top, for example the selection of a parliamentary candidate by the local party or the bid by a local authority for central government funding for a road expansion scheme, or from the top of the political structure toward all below. An example of the latter is economic policy decisions presented in the budget or local government decisions to use local taxpayers' money to provide recreational facilities.

Social and Economic Power

Society is defined, in brief, as either the sum of the people who live within a state or as a description of the groups, each identified by their own common characteristic within that state, and their interests and relations with other groups. Social power is (any) influence which a person or persons exercise which changes the characteristics of a group or its relations with other groups. Thus Salmon Rushdie's *Satanic Verses* brought about changed relations between the Muslim and non-Muslim communities in Britain. Any person or persons who, for example, change consumer habits among the group who have professional employment - by, shall we say, the purchase by members of that group of country cottages in Britain or France and the consequent changes in their leisure time activities and friends - have exercised social power.

Economics, in brief, describes the production and distribution of goods and services. (The same word - economics - is used for the academic discipline which studies and describes economic activity.) Economic power, therefore, is influence by a person or group of people on the production and distribution of goods and services. Influence on economic activity may be exercised at the national level by the government. For example, a change in Bank Rate will influence business decisions, such as a debate within a company on whether to proceed with plans to build a new production plant. Economic power can be exercised at the local level by local government, for example by a planning permission decision for a particular company, by managers with their arrangements for production - when to work, whether to employ more people - and by the workforce by, for example, their agreement to work practices or by their withdrawal of labour.

Many government decisions, exercises of political power, influence the economy and are thus also exercises of economic power but this is not so for all decisions: changes to the law on capital punishment is an example of the exercise of political power which will influence the social but not the economic sphere. Some decisions relate to the political, economic and also the social spheres. A change to the Sunday trading laws, by influence on the work and the leisure pattern of that group in society who are employed in shops, will be an exercise of political, economic and social power.

The Subject of History

It will be seen from this chapter that power, political, economic and social power, is central in national, local and even domestic life. Power, either formal or informal, as influence by others on you and by you on others is the stuff of our life in society and part of the give-and-take of relationships. Power, and an interest in power, is not malign. Unless a person's wish for power becomes so consuming that they seek domination, the ebb and flow of influence between people and groups of people is a reflection of active lives which generate the changes in the story of Man in society in the past which is the subject of history.

Gilbert Pleuger.

19 Society

During the early 1980s a Japanese soldier was found on a small Pacific island. Since 1945, unaware that the war had ended, he had lived off the land and remained in readiness to single-handedly defend the island against Japan's Second World War enemies. While it is possible to write a biography of this soldier's life since 1945, by itself it would not be a history because history is an account of Man *in society* in the past.

The concept of society, as used in 'the history of society'

(margin text, rotated): core concepts, terms and ideologies

or 'social history' has two levels of meaning. At one level, the word describes the sum of the people who live under the same government within the same state. At another level the word describes the groups within the state who are identified by a common characteristic or interest and the relation of that group with other groups within the state. In this latter sense a study of society requires that the historian subdivide the citizens of a state, for the purposes of study, into sub-society groups. Any criteria can be used for this subdivision. Among the more frequently used are wealth or income, type of employment, education, leisure activities, religion or political affiliation. It is possible to group the members of a state by the colour of their eyes, county of birth or consumption patterns. The terminology used by the mathematician for sub-groups is set and by the logician class. Karl Marx used the word class to describe the groups within society who were bound together by a common relationship to the means of production. Whatever criteria is used to identify a group, it is the distinguishing behaviour and views of the group and the relationship with other groups, which interests the historian. Over time there will be changes in the groups: these changes are described by the historian and the reasons for them and their consequences analysed.

In earlier centuries, before modern data collection, numerical information is ascertained with difficulty but from it such generalisation as 'the decline of the gentry', 'the rise of the middle classes' or 'the age of enterprise' are made by historians. Close comparison between one age and another, because of the use of different criteria, can be incomplete but two examples which illustrate the dynamic character of society are given below.

Category	1436	1696
Yearly average family income (£s)		
Temporal lords	768	2800
Knights	134	486
Esquires	24	450
Gentlemen	12	280
Richer freeholders	5.6	84

Sources: H.L. Gray, *English Historical Review*, 1934, J.P. Cooper, *English Historical Review*, 1967, and G.N. Clark, *The Wealth of England from 1496 to 1760*, OUP, 1946.

Occupational group	(per cent) 1911	1961
Employers and proprietors	6.7	4.7
White-collar workers	18.7	35.9
Managers and administrators	3.4	5.4
Higher professionals	1.0	3.0
Lower professionals	3.1	6.0
Foremen and inspectors	1.3	2.9
Clerks	4.5	12.7
Salespersons	5.4	5.9
Manual workers	74.6	59.3
Skilled	30.5	25.3
Semi-skilled	34.4	25.4
Unskilled	9.6	8.6

Source: A.H. Halsey (ed.), *Trends in British Society since 1900*, Macmillan, 1972.

Society is the more slowly moving and more tightly bound substrata, on the surface of which the 'events' of history happen. Changes in society bring interest, sometimes excitement, to historians as they discern the past's moving tableaux.

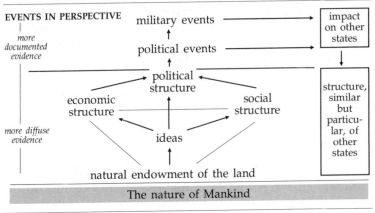

20 Absolutism

Stand on the Great Terrace at Versailles and look down the long vista of fountains, lakes and statues, framed by woods. Then turn and survey the massive sweep of the palace behind you. Pass through its great halls and enter the huge courtyard

Core concepts, terms and ideologies

dominated by the equestrian statue of the king by whom and for whom the whole edifice was built. Now go back in imagination and people it with ministers, courtiers, officials, soldiers, musicians and flunkeys: the court of the greatest monarch of the day. This was the Sun-King. Louis XIV stood then, as he does now, as the embodiment of Absolutism.

What is, or was, Absolutism? The word comes from the Latin *solvere* which means to loosen, untie or release. Sixteenth-century scholars writing in Latin often argued that a king must be *legibus solutus* which means 'unrestrained by the laws'. Hence such a monarch was said to be absolute 'in the sense that he commands but is never commanded, and so can never lawfully be opposed by any of his subjects.[1] His rule might, some theorists said, be justified by the Divine Right of Kings.

To define Absolutism is easier than deciding which monarchs were absolutist. For example, one historian (Perry Anderson) cites Habsburg Spain as the very model of Western European Absolutism, while another (Henry Kamen) denies that it was absolutist at all: I agree with Kamen.[2] The truth is that no monarch in the early modern period was absolutely absolute; each appears more or less so according to the particular characteristics emphasised. Still, Louis XIV, Frederick William and Frederick II of Brandenburg-Prussia, Peter the Great and Catherine the Great of Russia, Charles XI and Charles XII of Sweden are among those with a fair claim to absolute monarchy.

It is helpful to consider Absolutism, both in theory and in practice, as falling into two roughly equal periods: the first running from the early sixteenth to the mid-seventeenth century, and the second from mid-seventeenth century to the end of the eighteenth. The first was an age of conflict, much of it bound up with religion and culminating in the terrible Thirty Years' War (1618-1648). In this period, absolutist theory was in debate with constitutionalist theory; and, in practice, monarchs were in internal conflict with dissident nobles, estates or parliaments, provinces, and religious groups. In many countries (England, Scotland, Ireland, France, Spain/ Portugal, the Netherlands) these conflicts peaked about 1640-50. In the second period, constitutionalist theories in many countries gave way to enlightenment theories, which were as much supportive as critical of Absolutism - hence the phenomenon of Enlightened Despotism. In practice, religious conflicts came to an end, estates were either dispensed with or became empty formalities, and the aristocracies came into partnership (sometimes, as in France or Poland, a dominating partnership) with the monarchs.

The Crucible for Absolutism

What was the previous state of affairs from which Absolutism grew and with which, during the first of these periods, it was in conflict? It is known by its neat German name, *Ständestaat*, which means 'the state or society of corporations and estates'. In the twelfth and thirteenth centuries all aspects of civilisation advanced. Monarchies benefited from the growth of law, the authority given them by the influx of Roman law, and the development of able bureaucracies to carry out their policies. The growth of law and learning helped also to secure rights and privileges to many other groups in society: cities and towns, universities, guilds, cathedral chapters, societies of merchants, etc. But the chief beneficiaries of this age of legal and corporate privilege were the representative bodies or assemblies known as 'parliaments' in English, *états-généraux* in French, *cortes* in Spanish, and so on. Between about 1200 and 1500 they appeared in every realm in Latin Christendom. Usually they co-operated with, sometimes they opposed, the rulers; but no monarch at first could do without them.

Such assemblies were normally composed of 'houses' or 'estates' representative of the three 'orders' of clergy, nobles and towns. The rulers needed them for consultation over problems of war, justice, administration and, above all, taxation. Moreover, because of the legal privileges of so many corporations (boroughs, guilds, merchant companies, the Church, feudal vassals, provinces), the kings were largely dependent on these for providing soldiers, money, ships, courts of justice, law-enforcement, etc. Gradually, however, and with many false starts, the monarchs began to gather these powers into their own hands. Castile, where estates first appeared, was also (in the 1520s) the first kingdom to reduce them to subservience. Thereafter, once a monarch could tax without their permission, maintain a standing army and employ an effective bureaucracy, he could snap his fingers at his estates. This did not happen in England, the Netherlands, Poland, Hungary, Mecklenburg and Württemberg, but in most realms, by the end of the seventeenth century something like Absolutism had emerged.

Theorists of Absolutism

Finally, a word about the theorists. They fall into two groups: some, like Suarez, Bodin, Grotius, Hobbes, Pufendorf, argued, on rationalist and natural law bases, that absolute legislative sovereignty must be held by one man (or woman or, occasionally, group as in Venice). Others, like William Barclay, Sir Robert Filmer and Bishop Bossuet, added to this the religious theory of the divine right of kings, which argued (on the basis of Scripture, especially Romans XIII) that resistance to the king is tantamount to resistance to God.

In the end, the American and French Revolutions put a virtual end to Absolutism, though some monarchies tried to revive it after the fall of Napoleon. In the twentieth century Absolutism has been replaced by the much more sinister phenomenon of dictatorship, which, ironically, was born in the French Revolution, amid the death-throes of Absolutism.

Notes

1 Quentin Skinner, *The Foundations of Modern Political Thought,* Vol. 2, 1978, p. 287.

2 Perry Anderson, *Lineages of the Absolutist State,* 1979, pp. 60, 61; Henry Kamen, *Spain in the Later Seventeenth Century,* 1665-1700, 1980, pp. 17, 159.

Dr Michael Stanford.

21 Capitalism

'Capital' was coined around the twelfth century from the Latin term *caput* meaning 'head'. It meant any potentially profitable stock of goods or cash. Not till the seventeenth century do we find the term 'capitalist' used in its modern sense. The 'ism' was stuck on in the mid-nineteenth century.

It rather misleadingly implies that capitalism is a rigid or well-defined, never-changing 'system'; or that it began as a set of abstract ideas (an ideology) which was then imposed on society (like feminism, socialism, existentialism etc.) Generally speaking we are either for 'isms' or 'against' them. They can rarely be used in a neutral or descriptive manner. Capitalism, like feudalism, is one of those words which the historian must hedge with qualifications.

Nor is it an 'ism' in the sense that it is a system which is fixed in time. We cannot be precise about its exact meaning, let alone the point of 'take-off'. Capitalism evolved out of an attempt to solve certain problems in early medieval business practices with techniques of credit initially borrowed from the Arabs.

Knights of Gold

The Knights Templar were a crusading order who did not see themselves as entrepreneurial individualists. Their managers introduced new methods from the East to maximise the profit from their vast international empire of lands and castles. In this way they could generate income to finance future crusades without selling their capital. Because Europe at the time was ripe for expansion but acutely short of cash they soon became the first international bank. The new financial methods spread. First to the Christian banking houses of Italy and later to wherever western merchants set up business. When the order was dissolved (so that its assets could be confiscated by the French King) the inquisitors puzzled generations of future historians with the claim that the Christian knights confessed to worshipping a pagan idol or 'head.' This mysterious object was never found. For the true corruption of the Templars was not black magic but the fact that they had come to worship their *caput*, or financial capital, in place of Christ.

Marriage of Instinct and Method

But what is capitalism? How does it differ from the principle of buying cheap and selling dear, which has governed the lives of traders - successful or not - since neolithic times? Capitalism is not primarily about greed or even individual enterprise. If we read Homer we can see there was no shortage of either as early as 1000 BC. It would be nearer the mark to see capitalism as an application of scientific rationality to otherwise universal human instincts. Greed, need and conspicuous consumption were not created by capital. Rather they are the vantage points on which Capital weaves its ever-growing credit structure.

Self-generating Wealth

Capital is something which will generate a steady profit over the longest term possible. Capital is about minimising risk and maximising opportunity. Initially it can be small or gigantic; but it must trigger a process of self-generating wealth. How is it different from traditional money-lending? Firstly, it is not a one-to-one relationship. The transformation of wealth into capital depends on what we would nowadays call the creation of a reliable credit infrastructure. Cheques, Bills of Exchange, the discounting of bills, an international clearing system, paper money, stocks and shares, are all parts of a complicated alchemy that turns mere wealth (land, gold, cash, raw materials, manufactured goods) into Capital. In the money market money itself becomes the commodity. But the key element is to involve as many transactions and people as possible.

The creation of modern insurance, for example, is one of the elements which marks the transition to more scientific, risk-free forms of corporate financing. One result of all these ever-improving techniques is a financial (and perhaps social) climate of relative stability. Credit is relatively cheap and plentiful. Even the smallest enterprises can generate new wealth. A money lender's interest rates are as high as the borrower will accept (usury). Low interest rates (single figures) with a guaranteed return on capital investment are the hallmark of a stable credit system. Although wars certainly benefit some groups of capitalist they tend to destabilise this simple credit mechanism (notably in 1914): hence perhaps the Templars' increasing reluctance to go crusading.

core concepts, terms and ideologies

Capitalists' Trust

A fourteenth-century Italian, St Bernardino of Sienna wrote: 'What is Capital? It is like those hidden seeds, from which in the beginning God allowed created things to grow; particles of profit yet unborn, which grow by successive increments to an original rule.' This contemporary of the Medici bankers had grasped that the key was neither to be rich, nor to become rich, but to have the knack of discovering new seeds of wealth creation. Capitalism is perhaps best defined as 'manufacturing' wealth. It is the true philosopher's stone. The technical key to this process was (and remains) not alchemy but reliable instruments of credit. Credit (not land or money or manufactures) is the key to turning all these three things from static wealth into the seeds of a dynamic self-multiplying capital.

Reliability, honesty, co-operation and trust are the key things in the successful establishment of a system of credit. The greater the size of the credit system, the greater the ratio of paper (or plastic) to real wealth. This makes honesty all the more important. Naturally human nature guarantees plenty of exceptions. But throat-cutting, rampant individualism, fraud and violence would not (as St Augustine pointed out) make for good management on a pirate ship (let alone a bank). It is, on the whole, well-run respectable corporations, not maverick entrepreneurs, who have made capital into a world-mover.

Capitalist Dynamics

Capital is morally neutral. True to its original definition it is a calculus based on the head not on the heart. Maximising profit and minimising risk are its twin foci. But while mutual trust may be essential to business confidence, business confidentiality generates circles of initiates. Capital is sucked irresistibly into anything profitable. Politicians and drugs are just as much natural commodities as wine or bricks. Any business potentially less lucrative than its rivals is always at risk. Credit has been compared to a giant lung; it must breathe in as well as out. Hence the periodic phenomenon of slumps. The more deeply the world economy is penetrated by a single credit system the more spectacular and universal the potential downstroke.

There have always been controversial political and cultural 'baggage' associated with capital's natural tendency to grow and to self-globalise. Economic developments, combined with conscious policy-decisions, have ensured, since around 1700, that the world-wide trend of legislation has tended (despite reversals) to the creation of a social environment more favourable in every way to capital development than that prevailing in St Bernardino's day.

William Makin.

22 The *Ancien Régime*

The expression *'ancien régime'* (best thought of as 'former' rather than as 'old' regime) was invented by the French revolutionaries in their belief that they had given France an entirely new start, in terms of political and social structure, institutions and mental attitudes. It proved to be such a convenient form of shorthand for summing up a way of life that it passed into general currency and is often used by historians to describe European society as a whole, as it existed before the nineteenth century. Even a man like de Tocqueville, who saw the French Revolution as a process of acceleration rather than a change of direction, called his book *The Ancien Régime and the Revolution*. The term therefore encompasses both a description of a certain kind of society and a way of thinking about it.

Undivided Sovereignty

In its political aspect, *ancien régime* refers to a conception of monarchy in which the king claimed to rule by divine right, which meant that his power was theoretically absolute and he could not be called to account by any of his subjects, either individually or collectively. Since, as God's vice-regent, he was a legitimate ruler rather than a tyrant, he himself elected to exercise his authority in ways that were confirmed by

tradition and sanctified by the Gallican Church. This was
clear enough in principle. In practice it admitted of continual
argument between the king's Ministers and the custodians of
tradition, notably the parlements, which registered laws and
claimed the right to remonstrate against those that were
allegedly contrary to established practice, and by the Church.
The *ancien régime* therefore stood for an attitude of mind in
which sovereignty was undivided - the king was the ultimate
source of both legislation and the administration of justice -
and all forms of power were delegations of his supreme
authority. From this point of view, individual or collective
rights existed only to the extent that they constituted an
affirmation of traditional practices.

Diversity of Traditional Rights

Where institutions were concerned, the *ancien régime* was the
antithesis of uniformity. Over the centuries, individuals, collectivities like provinces and towns, and corporate bodies such
as law courts and trade guilds, had acquired 'liberties' or
immunities which they had come to regard as part of the
social fabric. The result was a patchwork quilt of almost
infinite variety: even within one small area there could be
many different weights and measures. In such a society,
politics usually took the form of an aggrieved defence of
what were claimed to be traditional corporate rights, against
any threat of encroachment by competing collectivities, the
Church in its temporal capacity, or the royal government. A
shared concept of legitimacy allowed, if it did not actually
generate, endless dispute about the way in which things
should be managed and the frontiers of local or corporate
power.
     The sanctity of tradition implied respect for hereditary
privilege. In a society where no one was a citizen, the
privileges of subjects were to a great extent determined by
their birth. This could confer advantages of various kinds,
such as the inheritance of office, but its most obvious
manifestation was in the existence of an order of nobility,
conceived as apart from the rest of the population, whose
behaviour was regulated by a code of honour that, in the last

resort, took precedence over obedience to the law. This separate identity of the *gentilhomme* (there is no English equivalent of equal power) was recognised by the king, in his capacity of 'first *gentilhomme* of the kingdom'. Nobility was essentially a matter of personal status, but that in itself implied certain privileges, such as serving the king at Court or as officers in his army and navy, and exemption from certain forms of taxation. In practice, such status was usually accompanied by privileges derived from feudalism, for example, those inherent in the lordship of manors, but the two were distinct and, in France, manorial rights were articles of commerce that could be bought by commoners. Nobility itself could be acquired by office, as well as by personal grant from the king. Socially speaking, the *ancien régime* can therefore best be considered, not as something totally static, but as a slow-moving escalator on which the more successful of the French king's subjects jostled for precedence in the hope of joining those whom, in the meantime, they were inclined to envy.

Forces of Change

Within this society, dedicated to the principle of stability, there were two main forces of change. The French economy expanded very quickly in the eighteenth century, mainly as a result of overseas trade. The immediate consequence of this was not the creation of a frustrated middle class, impatient for political power and social recognition. The *ancien régime* was flexible enough, for a time at least, to assimilate the successful. Nevertheless, the values of the market place were implicitly alien to it and there was an increasing tendency to contrast those who made a 'real' contribution to the prosperity of the country with the 'parasites' whose claim to preferential treatment rested on the services of their ancestors. Such attitudes tended to be reinforced by the sceptical rationalism induced by the beliefs of the Enlightenment. Scornful of tradition, as the survival of past superstition, and dedicated to the conviction that the social sciences could provide the key to good government and economic prosperity, the men of the Enlightenment held that everything -

politics, economics, social attitudes, the organisation of the Church - must be justified by results. Convinced of the existence of a rational, and for many of them, a Providential order, they believed that success in all fields was guaranteed if the correct policies were followed. Unsatisfactory performance must therefore be the fault of those whose ignorance or prejudice had led them to misuse power. It was an offence against reason that should not be allowed to continue. Like all phases of civilisation, the *ancien régime* consisted of a synthesis of attitudes derived from the past, confronted by forces of change external to its system of belief. During the eighteenth century these changes accelerated and the problem of assimilating them became more and more intractable.

Professor Norman Hampson.

23 Revolution

The newspaper storyline the other day read 'Venezuela Revolution Attempt Fails'. Almost every month a revolution or attempted revolution is reported somewhere in the world and the word revolution is used not only in connection with the control of government and with political events. People also speak of 'the green revolution', 'the electronic revolution', 'the cultural revolution' (Mao's inspired changes in China, 1968) and even 'the revolution in expectations'. Clearly revolution is a key concept in the contemporary world.

The Concept and its Evolution

Initially used to describe astronomical movement, in the later Middle Ages revolution was applied to a great change of circumstance in a situation, and by 1600 to describe the complete overthrow of a government. Political events in France in and after 1789 were called a revolution almost immediately and it was the vigour of these events, the extent to which people's lives were changed by them, the Europe-wide impact of the happenings in France and its continuing importance in the political life of the states of Europe which greatly increased the usage of the word. By the late nine-

core concepts, terms and ideologies

teenth century, and the increased pace of change in the economy and society of western states, revolution began to be used to describe changes in these areas. J.R. Green the late Victorian historian, for example, in his *A Short History of the English People,* 1874, has a chapter on the Agrarian and Industrial Revolutions.

Revolution always describes change. Even in its astronomical application the word is used to describe movement, that is change in position. While all revolutions involve change not all change can be described as revolution. That change that can be called a revolution must have characteristics which a (mere) change lacks. That which is particular to that class of change which warrants the different name *revolution* is either the *great speed* and/or the *great extent* of change or the *great number of people* affected and/or the *great degree* to which they are affected by change. This latter pair of characteristics more readily relates to social and economic change while the former more readily relates to political change. A society which urbanised very quickly, such as Stalin's Russia during collectivisation, is justly described as having undergone a social revolution.

Politics and Revolution

Analysis of political revolutions suggest a more complicated picture is possible. Peter Calvert in *A Study of Revolution,* Oxford University Press, 1970, starts with a definition of political revolution as 'a complete overthrow of the established government of a country or state by those who were primarily subject to it; a forcible substitution of a new ruler or form of government'. The emphasis here is on revolution as historical *events* but he accepts there are, within the area of revolution that we call political, other circumstances which can be called revolution namely:

- A *process* in which the political direction of a state becomes increasingly discredited in the eyes of either the population as a whole or certain key sections of it. *Such a process may culminate in the revolutionary event . . . or in the change of government by more peaceful means.*

- A more-or-less coherent *programme* of change in either the political or the social institutions of a state, or both, induced by the political leadership *after* a revolutionary event, the transition of power, has occurred.

- A political *myth* that gives to the political leadership resulting from a revolutionary transition short-term status as the legitimate government of the State.

Carl Leiden and Karl M. Schmitt in *The Politics of Violence: Revolution in the Modern World*, Prentice-Hall, 1968, classify revolutions under five heads: 1 mass. 2 millennial. 3 spontaneous. 4 conspiratorial. 5 militarised mass. Revolutions follow a wide variety of courses but Leiden and Schmitt nevertheless generalise the stages of revolution as: Stage 1 violence and the destruction of the existing regime. This stage will include: (a) the expulsion of the old ruling elite; (b) the breakdown of old loyalties; (c) the undermining of the old ideology. Stage 2 is the construction and replacement of (a), (b) and (c) in the first stage. Stage 3 is characterised by a reduction in the vigour of revolutionary activity and an increased wish to return to normalcy and a tendency toward the centralising of authority.

Beware of Marginal Cases

In one of my better undergraduate answers I questioned whether the events of 1905 in Russia warrant the description 'revolution'. Is it correct to describe the events in England in 1688 as a revolution as distinct from an invasion and is it always easy to distinguish between rebellion and revolution? Taking an example from social history, we may readily agree that there have been huge changes in the movement of people by air during this century and this has had considerable consequences in society, but it is less easy to agree when the revolution began: with the introduction of schedule services? With the use of jumbo jets? When the holiday industry had the capacity to accommodate the travellers? Unless the concept of revolution is applied with discrimination, and marginal cases treated with care, the concept will be devalued because of the loss of a sharpness of definition - rather as a photograph loses its value if it is poorly focused and appears smudged.

Gilbert Pleuger.

24 Liberalism

Liberalism, like the other ideologies which inform modern political thought and practice, is very much a product of the French Revolution. What we see in the Revolution is a concerted attempt to broaden the base of politics by mobilising the passive population. Political demands were advanced in a new idiom, directed beyond the old élite to groups whose involvement in politics had previously been negligible. Styles of argument which suited the narrow political world of the *ancien régime* were set aside as the Revolution gathered momentum, leading to modes of discourse that were at once more abstract and more inclusive, addressed to individuals as such rather than to members of estates, guilds or professions.

Revolutionary rhetoric reveals a new conception of what it means to be a member of a political community. The point is emphatically proclaimed in the *Declaration of the Rights of Man and the Citizen* (1789), where it is contended that 'men were born and remain free and equal', enjoying 'natural and imprescriptible rights', with a collective identity in the nation which constituted the only legitimate source of political authority.

Politics for the Individual

The stress on individual rights, with the legitimacy of a community being judged according to its capacity to facilitate the ends and ambitions of individuals, became a common property of nineteenth-century liberal thought. The term 'liberal' in the political sense only gained currency in Spain after 1810, where it was used to describe the position of groups which argued for constitutional restraint on government and freedom of expression. But it quickly became associated more generally with the defence of constitutional reform and individual freedoms.

If the term is recent, however, the basic philosophical

core concepts, terms and ideologies

building blocks of liberal thought have a long and distinguished pedigree. The roots of individualism can be traced in stoic and Christian thought and individualist assumptions informed Roman law. But the great flowering of individualism occurred in the early modern period. In the Reformation, for example, the priority of the individual's relationship with God was a basic tenet of theological controversy. And in the political sphere Hobbes (1588-1679), Locke (1632-1704) and a host of lesser figures based their theories of obligation and authority on the doctrine of natural rights. In the eighteenth-century reform movement it was simply taken for granted that the individual rather than the State was the focus of value. It was assumed that traditional practices and privileges could be subjected to rational scrutiny and rejected if they were deemed to be detrimental to individual well-being or fulfilment.

Liberalism and Constitutions

The shift from a group-centred to an individual-centred political philosophy, however, was by no means unambiguous in its practical implications. Strategies to defend and promote individual interests could range from the cautious model adopted in the United States in 1776 to the frenzied attempts to find a constitutional form appropriate for the realisation of liberty, equality and fraternity in France in 1792-3. Indeed the invocation of the guillotine in the defence of a regime which justified itself in terms of its promotion of natural rights terrified liberals themselves as France seemed to teeter on the brink of anarchy. Conservative and reactionary critics such as Burke (1729-97) and de Maistre (1753-1821) attributed the atrocities of the revolution to a false and shallow philosophy which rejected any restraints on individual assertion. The criticism, to be sure, was based upon a caricature of the doctrine of natural rights. But liberals were led to reappraise both their conceptions of the State and the scope for individual advancement.

A much more cautious and defensive style of liberalism emerged after 1815. Benjamin Constant (1767-1830), for example, sought to distinguish liberty within a constitutional

core concepts, terms and ideologies

core concepts, terms and ideologies

framework from direct popular involvement in the formation and implementation of policy. His concern was to distinguish the ideals of 1789 from the terror of 1793. A key theme, articulated classically by von Humboldt (1767-1835) and J.S. Mill (1806-73), became the insistence on a clear separation between public and private spheres. While Alexis de Tocqueville (1805-59) insisted that the defence of liberty and the pursuit of equality were mutually exclusive.

Attributing priority to the rule of law over the attainment of substantive goals gave liberalism a decidedly conservative tinge. It was one thing to leave individuals to pursue their own goals in life, but quite another to argue that radical inequality made no difference to people's actual options. As industrialisation and population growth gathered momentum, so it became clear that urgent social and economic problems would not be satisfactorily resolved if left to individual initiative. T.H. Green (1836-82), for example, championed a much more interventionist role for the State than had been the fashion among mid-century liberals. In the twentieth century liberals would feel able to make common cause with socialists across a whole range of issues, arguing that public provision of basic welfare and educational requirements was a necessary condition for individual fulfilment and contentment. Purists might argue that liberalism had strayed a long way from its roots. What had not changed, however, was its central preoccupation with the individual.

Dr Bruce Haddock. University College of Swansea.

25 Socialism

Socialism as a political movement was very much a response to the consequences of industrialization. Liberalism and capitalism emerged in socialist argument as Janus-faced villains, defending a conception of political and economic freedom which effectively perpetuated the subordination of the working classes. Socialists might not agree about precisely what was wrong with the *status quo;* nor could they necessarily agree on a common programme for the future. But there was a general consensus in socialist circles that the ideals of the

French Revolution - liberty, equality, fraternity - could not be attained in a political system built upon an individualist foundation.

Industrialisation and the Insufficiency of Individual Initiative

Industrialisation in the nineteenth century created both new possibilities for ordinary people and massive difficulties. It was widely held that complex problems of integration and control in the economy and society could not be left to individual initiative. In the early decades of the century arguments were being mooted urging a high degree of central control in economic planning. Robert Owen (1771-1858) and Saint-Simon (1760-1825), for example, contended that scientific and technical progress had created alternatives to capitalist production which were both more efficient and more humane. Problems which had in the past been treated as the 'natural' concomitants of human life - poverty, exploitation, crime - were, on this view, attributable to an outmoded social and economic system. Replace anarchic competition with rational planning, coercion in the factory with co-operation, and not only would productive capacity be increased but there would be no further need for the State to assume a repressive role.

Ideas of this kind were growing in popularity, especially among educated workers in London and Paris in the 1840s. They constituted a frame of reference in which substantive political, social and economic demands could be advanced - for universal male suffrage and annual parliaments among the Chartists, for a radical redistribution of property among the Paris workers. But, far-reaching though the practical implications of these demands might be, they were thoroughly reformist in tone. The contention was that by amending specific institutions and practices, wholesale benefits would accrue to working people. What transformed socialism into a deadly threat to the liberal order was the supposition that meaningful change could not be achieved within the confines of a capitalist system. Revolutionary socialists vested their hopes for the future in the dawning political awareness of the

concepts, terms and ideologies

working class. In their view, capitalism had created, along with unparalleled wealth, an impoverished and brutalised industrial proletariat. As the logic of their class position became clear, however, the proletariat would undergo a metamorphosis. The passive victims of capitalist exploitation would assume the direction of a new era.

Class-based Socialism

Karl Marx (1818-83) was the principal architect of a class-based socialism. In his early writings he targeted his criticism on the view, central to liberal theory, that moral and political principles have a universal validity. He argued, instead, that the view individuals form of their predicament (expressed in moral, political, philosophical, religious, aesthetic or whatever terms) was a product of their place in a complex of social and economic roles. Marx saw the ideological realm as a reflection of more fundamental conflicts and developments in the economy and society.

This shift of perspective involved a quite different conception of political argument. In *The Communist Manifesto* (1848) Marx sought to raise the revolutionary consciousness of the industrial proletariat by explaining the economic basis of their new-found political strength. In later, more systematic works, he went on to argue that the internal contradictions of capitalism would precipitate its collapse. In *Capital* (1867) Marx broke new ground in economic history by charting in detail the development and prospective demise of capitalism. But his researches were always guided by a political goal: the demonstration of the inevitability of the triumph of the proletariat.

Marx's specific predictions were not, of course, to be realised. The revolution which he had confidently expected in 1848 receded in his later writings to a more distant prospect. Nor can it be said that the states which have proclaimed themselves to be 'Marxist' in the twentieth century emerged in quite the way Marx had anticipated. But the fact remains that Marxism signally extended the range of political debate, furnishing a theoretical framework which facilitated the emergence of an organised labour movement.

The impact of Marxism is best measured in terms of the breadth of its appeal. Groups which would not describe themselves as Marxist could profit from the new emphasis on the politics of labour. Nor was Marx's direct legacy uniformly revolutionary. Soon after his death in 1883, leading intellectuals (Labriola and Croce in Italy, Sorel in France, Bernstein and Lassalle in Germany) were debating the practical implications of Marx's theories. It became evident that, when due attention was given to particular political contexts, Marxism could be used to justify an evolutionary as well as a revolutionary road to socialism. What had originally been presented as the doctrine of a small revolutionary sect could, by the 1890s, function as the theoretical foundation for a broad-based ideology, embracing a multitude of diverse groups and associations.

A plethora of socialisms has emerged in the twentieth century, some of them directly repudiating the Marxist heritage. Indeed the classic divide between communists and social democrats sets socialists in opposed political camps. What socialists share, however, is a rejection of a narrowly political view of freedom, contending instead that the eradication of wider economic and social constraints is a necessary condition for human fulfilment and wellbeing.

Dr Bruce Haddock. University College of Swansea.

26 Class

A class is a group of humans defined so as to suit the convenience of any given historical enquiry.

All you have to be able to do is to define the group you are talking about and explain why they are important enough to be singled out. You may perhaps get away with a brief reference to 'the hard-faced men who had done well out of the war'. But if you are unable to put a name to any of them; let alone discuss the average percentage profit on munitions contracts or the price of a peerage you are on shaky ground. Even greater caution applies to 'the rising middle class', 'the declining gentry', 'the new nobility', 'the rising and/or declining yeomanry' etc. There are also groups that go in pairs:

'court and country', 'ins and outs', 'York and Lancaster', 'Whigs and Tories', 'Gladstone and Disraeli'. A safe rule here is to warn the reader against simplistic polarisation, based on didactic mythologies, and pass quickly on.

The Origin of Class in Statistics

If you really do know what you are talking about, and can give precise examples such as 'Guy Fawkes, unemployed fireworkmaker, whose tailoring bill (unpaid) for ruffs alone was ten pounds, with a substantial mortgage on his coopering business, was typical of a whole class of fall guys/declining ruff traders/unemployed conspirators/rising/declining yeomen. (Strike out classes which do not apply.) Even so you are still in the position of *extending one individual case to a whole class.* You will need some broader statistics (score points here by drawing attention to possible sampling errors) and can round off with a mention of recent PhD research/articles into the role of fireworkmakers in selected county communities. What matters is that the student shows awareness that each society, and each group within it, is an anatomy with its own peculiar internal structure.

The inventors (so to speak) of class as a general explanation of historical events were Thucydides and Aristotle, way back in 400-300 BC. Karl Marx, their most distinguished disciple, was mainly an economist.

Incredibly Marx nowhere defines what class (central to his theory of class struggle) really means. The key sentence runs: 'What is class? Nothing could be simpler, or more necessary, than to answer this question.' Then, apparently, one of the maids (well scrubbed and smelling of carbolic soap) came in with the tea, or to dust down the antimacassars. Marx took time out to do some field work on the sexual mores of the servant class and the MS was never resumed. Chance may, after all, be the decisive factor in history.

Avoid off-the-top-of-the-head generalisations about any group. If a group is really important in your argument have a working definition and a cocktail of evidence in reserve. Even if you do not cite all this in full it will be clear to your reader that you have thought things through. Even eminent his-

torians have been unable to resist the lure of glib stereotypo-
logy: 'Junker mentality', 'broad-shouldered JPs laden with
stacks of statutes', 'fatalistic Castilians', 'rapacious Flemings',
'broad acred Whig squirearchs', or even 'hard-faced men who
had done well out of the whore' (class of 1540). If glibness
comes naturally then try politics. The professional historian
(even if his focus is mainly political) tries to build up a
mental picture (a sort of working model) of the society under
study. There is a textbook example of how this should be
done in Macaulay's famous third chapter to his *History of
England.* Macaulay talks about 'orders' or 'elements' or 'class'
promiscuously; but there is no doubt what he means.

You could make a start by trying to form a picture of
all the social groups mentioned by name in your current
textbooks. If you find you know less than you thought, you
may need to consult something more advanced. What was the
composition of these groups? Their legal status? Wealth and
occupations? The strains and tensions between (or within
them)? How did they fit together in one society? This will
then raise other questions, depending on your period. Some
think that in early modern or medieval history it is more
helpful to talk about orders rather than class. (You might
score points by asking teacher exactly what the difference is.)
Others think that class appeared only after the industrial
revolution. As the cold war drew to its climax in the 70s and
80s the pendulum swung rather sharply against class. Some
historians are against class and social history altogether. They
tend to ramble on about how they know everyone in the past
(who matters) by name.

Deliberate Divisions to help the Historian

These are not matters of fact but strategies for exploration. At
the end of the day analysis by class is very far from satellite
photography. Its more like the wide-meshed grid archaeologists use to highlight areas of interest on a mass of evidence.
Our grid is not going to be the same as the people used at
the time; though there will be important overlaps. One very
interesting question, which textbooks often leave unanswered,
is how contemporaries themselves thought about class. Two

core concepts, terms and ideologies

excellent books about the English class system are Jane Austen's *Persuasion* (especially chapters 1 and 2) and Charles Dickens' *Bleak House* (especially chapters 28 and 40). Shakespeare, Gogol and Tolstoy were keen observers too.

My own view is that much of the sound and fury about class in history has been party political. Perhaps the dust will now be allowed to settle. As Humpty Dumpty pointed out: 'A word means exactly what I want it to mean'. The central idea is that a class is not an object or a person which causes this or that. It is a segment or cut which the historian makes along what is really a social continuum. The idea is not to find ultimate answers but to look for new angles on an old problem or explore new methods of research.

William Makin.

27 Imperialism

In everyday language 'imperialism' tends to be a vague term with implications that often make it an epithet of rather indiscriminate abuse. Yet it is still a term that students of history should not be afraid of using, provided they do so with some care.

The Exercise of Power Over Another State or People

In a general sense 'imperialism' means the exercise of power by one state or one people over another. Thus it is perfectly acceptable to talk about the expansion of ancient Rome at the expense of its neighbours as 'Roman imperialism' or to talk about 'Spanish imperialism' in America in the sixteenth century. In this generalised sense 'imperialism' can often mean the creation of empires, that is, the subjugation of peoples by conquest and the creation of systems of foreign rule. Conquest and rule are, of course, the exercise of power in the most direct and obvious way. But power can be exercised in other, less direct, ways: historians are interested in phenomena that they call 'economic imperialism' or even 'cultural imperialism'. The dominant position that industrial Britain enjoyed for much of the nineteenth century or the

huge disparities between western countries or Japan in their
dealings with 'third-world' countries in modern times are
sometimes said to have created relations of economic imperialism in which the rich can impose their will on the poor.
Similarly, powerful, self-confident cultural movements, such as
missionary christianity or the modern film industry, may be
able to make powerful inroads into the cultural life of other
societies. Any attempt to apply the term 'imperialism' to
coercion beyond actual physical force does, however, require
caution. If the word is to mean anything, it is necessary to be
able to show that domination has been effectively exercised.
Trading relations or cultural exchanges between the strong
and the weak are not necessarily imperialistic, since they may
rest on relatively free choice. Strong states may wish to
manipulate apparently weaker states without directly ruling
them, and thus exercise what is sometimes called 'informal
imperialism' over them. But effective manipulation can be
very difficult to achieve.

The 'Age of Imperialism'

The term 'imperialism' came into use in the later nineteenth
century and for many historians the years from the end of the
nineteenth century to some point in the early twentieth
century are the classic 'age of imperialism' for the European
powers. This was a period in which existing empires, notably
those of Britain, France and Russia, greatly expanded and
new empires were created by Germany, the United States and
Japan. But claims that this was an age specially characterised
by imperialism usually depend less on the quantities of
people or territory incorporated into empires (which were not
especially notable by comparison with some other periods)
than of the attitudes to overseas expansion shown by the
western societies and their governments.

In Britain in the 1870s and 1880s those like Disraeli, who
were thought to be excessively committed to the use of force
abroad and to boasting about the extent of empire, were
dubbed 'imperialists' by their critics. Sections of opinion in
most western countries were indeed becoming increasingly
committed to beliefs that expansion overseas was fundamental

core concepts, terms and ideologies

to their national wellbeing. Various benefits were anticipated from programmes of imperialism: for some it was wealth from overseas trade and investments, for others it was power from the control of territory, for yet others it was moral improvement from the spread of culture and 'civilising' missions overseas. The extent to which the expectations behind such beliefs were ever fulfilled or western publics as a whole were ever committed to them is very debatable indeed; but there can be no doubt that highly competitive attitudes to overseas expansion had an important influence on European politics in the late nineteenth century. It is reasonable to call such attitudes 'imperialistic' ones and thus, while recognising their probable limitations in practical terms, also to accept conventional descriptions of this period as 'an age of imperialism'.

Imperialism and Overseas Business

A further specialised use of the term 'imperialism' developed at the end of the nineteenth century. This was a use particularly associated with economic expansion. The assumption behind this use of the term was that economic motives underlay the drive for domination overseas. Certain business or financial interests, whose profits depended on securing new outlets abroad, were said to be very powerfully entrenched in western societies at this time. Programmes of imperialism thus essentially reflected their needs. This line of argument was taken up by writers in the Marxist tradition, especially by Lenin who, in a famous pamphlet simply called *Imperialism* of 1916, described 'imperialism' both as a stage in the development of capitalism, when the great banks and other financial interests have become dominant, and as the practice of attempting to divide up the world between the countries where such interests were particularly powerful. Non-Marxist historians have rarely been able to accept in full either that western economies were as Lenin described them or the very heavy weighting given to certain economic interests as the explanation for imperial enthusiasm and expansion in Marxist historiography. Nevertheless, for many who use the term, 'imperialism' is still primarily related to the activities overseas of business interests.

Imperialism therefore, like so many historians' terms, has both general and specific meanings. It can be used generally to describe a phenomenon that exists at any time in human history: domination over others, exercised either directly through foreign rule or by indirect means. Imperialism has, however, come also to be associated with a particular period, from the late nineteenth century onwards. Its use then is rather diffuse, being applied both to the practice of domination overseas, and at home to attitudes, political programmes and, for some historians, primarily to developments within the economies of the major powers and the consequences that followed from these developments.

Professor Peter Marshall. King's College London.

28 Communism

Communism in its modern form is generally regarded as an off-shoot from socialism. Yet communist ideas, stressing the complete dependence of individuals upon the community and the abolition of private property, can be traced back to early Greek and Christian thought. Plato argued in the *The Republic* that his ruling class of philosopher guardians should enjoy a communal life style which freed them from the distraction of private interests and responsibilities; while early Christians and later monastic groups looked upon material possessions in relation to a more fundamental commitment to God.

Economy, Society and Modern Communism

What transformed communist theory in modem times is its relation to a wider analysis of society and politics. Communal living, which in the monastic ideal was an optional alternative to the depravity of civil society, became a necessary means for the eradication of injustice and inequality. Babeuf (1760-97) traced all that was unsatisfactory in society to the personal dependence of individuals upon one another. And that dependence would only be ended with the abolition of private property. In Babeuf's scheme of things it followed that if individuals had the same needs, they should necessarily enjoy the same facilities and benefits from society.

Marx gave communist theory a decisive twist by insisting that communism was not a more or less desirable mode of social and political organisation but an inevitable outcome of historical development. He continued to argue that private property and the division of labour stunted the prospects of individuals. What was novel in his argument, however, was the contention that such institutions constituted obstacles to further material progress. Particular modes of social organisation would ultimately fracture as a developing technology engendered new institutions and practices. In Marx's view, collective ownership and direction was a fitting reflection of the complex interrelationships of industrial society.

Marx, Lenin, Communism and Coercion

Problems within the Marxist tradition stem from the inadequacy of Marx's analysis of revolution. His expectation in the 1840s that revolution was imminent was tempered in his later writings. But he continued to argue that the establishment of communism would mark the end of coercive political institutions. The State, as an instrument of class rule, would wither away in a classless society. Marx was remarkably imprecise, however, about how the transition from capitalism to communism would occur. As the prospect of a cataclysmic revolutionary resolution waned, so Marx introduced the notion of a temporary 'dictatorship of the proletariat' which would control the allocation of resources until such times as the last vestiges of bourgeois society had been eradicated. The idea was exploited by Lenin (1870-1924), who insisted on the need for a vanguard party of the proletariat to assume the direction of affairs in order to raise the political consciousness of workers and peasants. A revolutionary élite had essentially furnished itself with an exquisite justification for authoritarian rule, much as had occurred with the Jacobins in the revolutionary upheavals in France after 1789.

Dictatorship of the proletariat has now become a synonym for tyranny. Marx's original usage, however, presupposed that capitalism had actually solved the problem of scarcity and that the vestiges of the bourgeois state's coercive functions would only be necessary in the transitionary period in which the ruling communist party needed to exploit the skills and services of individuals accustomed to the practices of the old regime. Marx's analysis of scarcity was mistaken. But so too was Lenin's expectation that revolution in Russia would trigger wider revolutionary upheavals in the more developed European states. Instead the Soviet Union found itself confronted by a hostile international environment. Defence of the revolution involved the perpetuation of an elaborate coercive apparatus. Under Stalin (1879-1953) the regime was finely tuned for both mass mobilisation and oppression. It proved incapable, however, of responding to the domestic needs of its people.

In the post-war period, the regime became increasingly bureaucratic. Central direction of the economy proved to be inefficient, leading to major problems as administrative, political and military costs grew. Attempts to reform the system by Gorbachev after 1985 precipitated a dramatic collapse in 1991.

Open door for Egalitarian Ideology

Communism as an ideology should not be identified with the Soviet regime. Western European communist parties, particularly in Italy, Spain, Portugal and France, have sought to fashion distinctively national roads to socialism, distancing themselves from Soviet policy and defending political alliances with wider groups as a means of fostering structural reform. With the demise of Soviet communism, however, the entire movement was dealt a decisive blow. Some parties sought to refashion themselves in order to bolster their parliamentary credentials. In doing so they largely severed their connections with the movement identified with Marx and Lenin, without necessarily establishing a clear ideological identity within their national traditions. For the moment, the communist chapter in modem political history appears to be closing, though it is certain that radically egalitarian ideologies will re-emerge in another guise.

Dr Bruce Haddock. University College Swansea.

29 Liberal Democracy

Democracy is a dominant aspiration for the peoples of Eastern Europe and the same goal is widespread throughout the non-western world. In *The Republic* Plato wrote:

'I dare say that a democracy is the most attractive of all societies,' I said. 'The diversity of its characters, like the different colours of a patterned dress, make it look very attractive. Indeed,' I added, 'perhaps most people would for this reason, judge it to be the best form of society, like women and children when they see gaily coloured things.'

Earlier in the same chapter Plato wrote '. . . democracy originates when the poor win, kill or exile their opponents and give the rest equal civil rights and opportunities of office, appointment to office being as a rule by lot.'

In these words Plato, although writing from the experience of the Greek city state, suggests the attractiveness of democracy and gives a better indication of the constitution of democracy than the simplistic clichés, 'one man, one vote' and 'government by the people, for the people'.

The Characteristics of Democracy

If we are to accurately communicate our ideas, a more complete description of what is meant by democracy is needed. Were the Levellers of the 1640s believers in democracy, or greater social and economic equality? Did the 1832 Reform Act initiate democracy or, if not, make an important step towards it? The concept of democracy, as an ideology and as a form of government, cannot be encapsulated in a short phrase. A description needs to specify its characteristics as a form of government, the attitudes widely held in common in a democratic society and the socio-economic conditions needed for democracy. The central characteristics of democracy are limitation of government and government by and within the law. In addition, there will be regular and peaceful change of government together with an elected

core concepts, terms and ideologies

institution to represent the electors and the electors will be given a genuine choice between candidates. This will require open analysis and discussion of questions which will, thereby, both inform the opinion of the electors and enable opinion to change. This latter characteristic is furthered by the absence of substantial restrictions on the freedom of speech, association and assembly. Although these characteristics point to the central constitutional and procedural features of democracy, in the absence of 'democratic' attitudes and socio-economic conditions, they are insufficient to ensure the vitality and survival of a democracy.

The Democrat's Society and Its Members

Without certain attitudes, held in common within a society, the continuance of the operation of a democracy is threatened. These attitudes include tolerance for other people's point of view, respect for minority and individual rights and the absence of fixed goals or a 'scientific' ideology such as racism or Marxism, as distinct from ideals generated within society to which to strive. Democracy, in contrast particularly to totalitarian government, is centred on individuals, their goals and ideals and their self fulfilment and, as a corollary, limited government interference is an aim.

Furthermore, it is clear democracy will not flourish even if members of a country wish to establish it, in the absence of particular socio-economic conditions. A democracy needs an organised public opinion and a public opinion which accepts the democratic procedures and accepts the authority of the government. A degree of industrialisation and an active media, to enable there to be national news and expressions and discussions of opinions, is needed if there is to be organised public opinion. Political parties, working within the arena of public opinion, foster political interest and further inform the electorate on the political issues as well as co-ordinate support. Lastly, any unassimilable minority, whether racial or tribal, economic or religious, is a threat to the consensus of assumptions which underlie the democratic society and its government.

It is these conditions and the role of a wide consensus

core concepts, terms and ideologies

of attitudes to underpin the formal arrangements of government, as well as the need to knit individual wishes into the
web of society, which make democracy vulnerable to dangers
from within and, thereby, from without.

Gilbert Pleuger.

30 Fascism

Fascism was a term generally applied to authoritarian
nationalist movements which developed in Europe after the
First World War. It was first used in Italy where Mussolini
founded the Italian Fascist Party in 1921. The name 'fascist'
came from the party's symbol, the bundle of rods and axes,
or *fasces*, carried as a sign of authority in ancient Rome. But
the term came to be applied generally to any movement that
preached intense nationalism and racism, popular dictatorship
and violent anti-Marxism. The National Socialist movement in
Germany under Adolf Hitler was the most successful fascist
party outside Italy, but there were small fascist parties in
most European states, in America and in Japan.

Fascism, like liberalism and socialism, had no single text
or body of thought that defined it. There were clear differences of emphasis between national fascist movements.
Many fascists saw the movement as deliberately anti-theoreti-
cal, and they stressed its active, violent character rather than
doctrine. Nevertheless, fascist movements generally shared a
common outlook on political organisation and social aims.
Fascist writers liked to think that they offered a 'third way',
and alternative path of development to bourgeois liberalism
on the one hand, or revolutionary socialism on the other.

Nationalism and Authoritarian Politics

The most distinctive feature of fascist movements was
nationalism. This often took the form of overt racism, for
fascists believed that the most authentic form of the national
state was one where people shared a common blood and a
common culture. National Socialists argued that racial conflict
was at the root of history itself, and that racial survival

depended on creating a pure racial state, with all alien or physically defective elements stamped out. Fascists insisted that the nation or race counted above all else, and that individualism, on which liberals placed such store, should be suppressed in favour of complete subordination to the wider needs of the state or the 'racial community' (*Volksgemeinschaft*).

To achieve a strong and united nation, fascists favoured an authoritarian political structure. The State would be ruled by a charismatic leader, a dictator whose word was law. The fascist movement itself would dominate public affairs, instituting a strict hierarchy of authority in all areas of life, and stamping out all political opposition. Fascists sought a new kind of élite to replace those based on wealth or privilege, made up of strong personalities, whose political skills and claims to leadership were forged in the 'struggle of life'. The fascist movement was designed to embrace all areas of life, from the level of the State, right down to culture, education and the family. Mussolini coined the term 'totalitarian' to describe fascist society, in the sense that it organised society 'totally'.

Fascism and Capitalist Society

Fascists believed that the nation was weakened by class conflict, and blamed capitalism for dividing society and creating antagonism with the workforce. Many fascists were opposed to capitalism as represented by big banks, industrial giants and international finance. They did not oppose private property as such - since most of their supporters were small owners of one kind or another - but they disliked the power exercised by big business and the social consequences of rapid industrial modernisation. In place of class they emphasised national solidarity, or the 'socialism of the race', as Hitler called it. Fascists were in favour of organising society on corporate lines, uniting workers and employers, farmers and labourers, in special corporations which were supposed to represent the interests of all, rich or poor. Though fascists tended to emphasise the importance of traditional family life, and lauded the virtues of simple peasant communities, they were not opposed to the modern world. What they wanted was to control modernisation so that it would serve the interests of the whole people, rather than creating social divisions and undermining national culture.

The Acceptance of Violence

To achieve these ends fascists were prepared to use any methods. Fascism has always been associated with violence, directed against the political enemies of the movement, or against racial 'undesirables' or in the wider racial struggle between different nations. Mussolini and Hitler both thought that imperialism and war were eternal features of history, and that the task of fascism was to instill military virtues into the population so that it would fight when it needed to. Mussolini dreamed of creating a new Roman Empire in the Mediterranean region, and in Africa. Hitler wanted a vast Eurasian empire stretching from the Rhine to the Urals, on which he could base his 'Thousand Year Empire'.

All of these things, the extreme nationalism and racism, the totalitarian rule of the party and its leader, the corporativist organisation of society, the imperative to violence, were the hallmarks of inter-war fascist theory. It was not always possible to put these ideas into practice. Once in power fascism had to compromise with other social groups, or had to accept that the fascist revolution in social and political life would take time. But in Hitler's Germany a great deal was achieved in twelve years, and the destruction of the European Jews and the German invasion of the Soviet Union showed how far Nazi leaders were prepared to go to impose their fantastic vision of racial cleansing and violent empire-building.

Professor Richard Overy. King's College London.

31 Totalitarianism

The events of 1989 in Eastern Europe were remarkable for a number of reasons. Communist rule crumbled or was overthrown, and even in the Soviet Union (as it then was) relatively free elections to the Congress of People's Deputies were held for the first time. Totalitarianism, it was often noted, had finally been vanquished within Europe and Francis Fukuyama was able to proclaim the 'end of history' in the sense that the principle of liberal democracy now stood unchallenged and seemed unlikely to be superseded (*The End of History and the Last Man*, Penguin Books, 1992). Totalitarianism, the scourge of European political life during the twentieth century, had suffered a final defeat with the collapse of its left-wing variant, the right-wing form having already been expunged with the defeat of the Axis power in the 1940s. But it was a long time adying and seemed to bracket together some rather diverse situations - the seediness of Hungary in the last years of Kadar's rule was certainly based on a system that differed from Western democracy but it was also distant from the ferocity of Nazi dictatorship (or even that of Joseph Stalin).

Totalitarianism was, then, a rather fuzzy concept - a feature by no means minimised by the fondness that right-wing politicians had for it as a term of political abuse (Ronald Reagan and Margaret Thatcher having made considerable use of it as recently as the 1980s). In fact its initial usage was generally positive. Leonard Schapiro in his book *Totalitarianism* (Macmillan, 1972) suggests as its originator Italian philosopher and fascist Giovanni Gentile, who used it in 1925 to describe a socio-political system that was comprehensive and all-embracing. It was soon taken up by Benito Mussolini who liked the undertones of vigour and massiveness it seemed to convey (if you try pronouncing it loud in Italian you can get some idea of what he meant). The term was not greatly favoured or even used in Nazi Germany, while Soviet authorities reserved it solely for fascist regimes and greatly resented its application to the Soviet Union and related communist regimes, regarding it as an ideological slur and an instrument of cold war propaganda.

There was, indeed, more than a little truth in this. It is significant, for example, that the most notable attempt to systematise the use of the term in political science, drawing and enlarging on similarities between Nazi Germany and Soviet Stalinism, was made in the early 1950s as cold war tensions strengthened and an anti-communist hysteria gripped much of American life. US scholars Carl Friedrich and Zbigniew Brzezinski formulated on this basis a 'totalitarian syndrome'. First outlined in their *Totalitarian Dictatorship and Autocracy* (Praeger, 1956), the syndrome had six features:

1 An official ideology to which general adherence was demanded, the ideology intended to achieve a 'perfect final stage of mankind'.

2 A single mass party, hierarchically organised, closely interwoven with the state bureaucracy and typically led by one man.

3 Monopolistic control of the armed forces.

4 A similar monopoly of the means of effective mass communication.

5 A system of terroristic police control.

6 Central control and direction of the entire economy.

It is possible to see on this basis the major similarities that could be detected between the classic modern dictatorships of Hitler and Stalin - and to understand why the played-out authoritarian regimes of 1980s Eastern Europe could also be placed in the same category. Despite abundant evidence of the failure of Marxism-Leninism as an ideological force and guide to the future, for example, none of the East European leaders were able to step outside its confines, communist parties clung on to their monopolistic power, economic reform was timid and unable to break with traditions of central control, and the mass media remained subject to party censors. It may have been 'totalitarianism with its teeth knocked out', as Polish writer and political activist Adam Michnik put it, but there were still residues of most of the features of the original syndrome. Although not on the scale of the police terror unleashed under Stalin and Hitler there were also cases like the murder of Polish priest Jerzy Popieluszko and the umbrella-tip poisoning of Bulgarian writer Georgi Markov, not to mention the gruesome Ceausescu tyranny in Romania and insistent 'normalisation' in post-invasion Czechoslovakia, to evoke the violence and persecution that underlay what, unfortunately, has to be regarded as a unique twentieth-century contribution to the vocabulary of political life.

Dr Paul Lewis. The Open University.

32 Nationalism

Nationalism as a political force emerged on the European scene with the French Revolution. We find nationalists aligned on both sides in the revolutionary struggles and wars of 1789-1815. But no matter what constitutional form nationalists might favour, they occupy common ground in their insistence that the identity of the nation confers value upon the State. In terms of its capacity to mobilise populations, nationalism is clearly the most effective of our modern ideologies. Taking the longer view of modern European history, it may be that the spectra of the French nation at arms will loom larger in significance than the specific goals the revolutionary armies were pursuing.

The roots of nationalism, however, should be sought beyond the sphere of politics. It had initially emerged in the eighteenth century as a reaction against the predominance of French culture in the literary world. In the minds of most intellectuals France and the Enlightenment had been identified as the acme of civilisation and refinement. Yet to critics such as Herder (1744-1803), French cultural supremacy was viewed as intellectually and morally ruinous. Enlightenment thinkers had tended to adopt an abstract, generalising vocabulary, blind to the subtle distinctions and nuances embedded in local cultural traditions. What made matters worse was that German or Italian or Czech writers were being encouraged to couch their work in an idiom and style which derived essentially from France. Peoples were being alienated from their roots. The only way to halt the decline was to foster local cultures. In the view of most nationalists, it was language, above all, that distinguished national cultural units. Individuals identified with their language at the most basic level. A cultural or political programme which countenanced neglect of so much that was important to them ran the risk of moral and intellectual atrophy.

National Identity and Self-government

A concern with roots and identity became a leading theme in nineteenth-century nationalist writings. The stress was on cultural diversity, language, shared myths and traditions rather than on specifically political categories. What transformed nationalism into a political movement was the reaction against the attempt to return to a system of dynastic politics in 1815. Peoples had grown accustomed to new styles of political thought and practice and new loyalties had emerged. Problems were most acute within the sprawling Austrian Empire. Educated Slavs, Hungarians or Italians simply could not identify with rule from Vienna. Within these suppressed nations (for that is how they began to regard themselves) movements arose with a very clear political objective - to rid the nation of foreign rule. The ideal of national self-government was thrust to the forefront of political debate, with the question of the kind of constitutional arrangement which might be appropriate for a community being treated as a secondary issue.

The most striking representative of this new style of nationalism was Giuseppe Mazzini (1805-72). His nationalism had a specifically political focus. Yet he shared many of the assumptions which had informed Herder's view. He rejected abstract 'scientific' analysis of history and society, focusing instead on identification with the non-reflective attitudes and dispositions which are the foundation of a way of life. What mattered to him was not so much that individuals should be enabled to pursue their particular interests but that they should be aware of the ties which bound them to their communities.

Ideology for Liberation or for Repression and War

Nationalism assumed the guise of a liberation movement in response to the challenge of imperial rule. As a political movement, however, it embraced a variety of positions, ranging from radical claims for direct democracy to defence of

core concepts, terms and ideologies

the most extreme forms of authoritarianism. This flexibility, of course, was essential to the appeal of the movement. Nationalists could set their ideological or constitutional differences aside in a common commitment to the contention that communities with a sense of their own linguistic or cultural identity should have a political voice. Here were tantalising possibilities for established authorities. Through identification with the State as a symbol of the nation, a sense of political participation could be attained without any real extension of popular involvement in government. Nationalism could thus generate from within its own resources a remarkable transfiguration from an ideology of liberation to the official doctrine of a repressive state.

There had, indeed, always been a darker side to the history of nationalism. Fichte (1762-1814), for example, saw the nation in such exclusive terms that a national state would be justified in pressing its claims not only against other states but against dissenting voices amongst its own people. The bond between people who spoke a common language was regarded as so crucial to their fulfilment that nothing could be allowed to distract them from their sense of common purpose. With the leaven of social Darwinism later in the century, these ideas would warrant the most aggressive policies. Nations could be pictured maximising their moral and political energies in competition with one another, with individuals subordinating their interests, and sometimes their lives, to the pursuit of a common good. Once the interests of the State had been identified with the needs of the nation, it was but a small step from a view of a world of diverse nations, each finding a political outlet for their energies, to that of a world in which a nation is justified in asserting itself against other nations. What had originally been conceived as a recipe for international harmony and co-operation could be transformed into a pretext for imperial adventures and war.

Dr Bruce Haddock. University College Swansea.

The Student
and Evidence

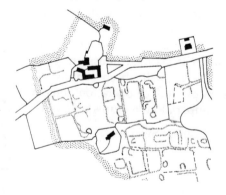

33

Evidence and the Historian

Historical Statements are not Self-evident

IN AN ARTICLE in *History Sixth* by Richard Brown and Christopher Daniels on 'Working with Sources' they emphasise that 'the basis of good documentary work is an understanding of the value and limitations of the available evidence.' Perhaps it is worth spending a little time in considering this very important thing called 'evidence'.

I begin with a few simple propositions:
1 All bachelors are unmarried.
2 Two times two is four.
3 349 times 131 = 45,719.
4 Water is a combination of hydrogen and oxygen.
5 Everest is about 29,000 feet high.
6 Elizabeth I, the last Tudor monarch, desired the death of Mary, Queen of Scots.
7 The 'Guildford Four' were not guilty of a bombing outrage.
8 Liberal democracy is preferable to Communism.
9 I have a pain in my left knee.
10 It is raining.

Of these, numbers 1, 2, 9 and 10 (if true) are clearly true. They have no need of evidence to support them; on the contrary, they are themselves evident, the sort of propositions that might be evidence for others. Number 3 is not evident, though it is necessarily true for the same reason (mathematical) that number 2 is. It stands not so much in need of evidence as of demonstration. Number 4 is true at all times and all places; we may say that it is universally true, but not necessarily true. We need experimental evidence for its truth, though most people would accept it without this. Number 5 is also contingently, not necessarily, true, and we need the evidence of measuring instruments. The remaining three, numbers 6, 7 and 8, are quite different. They are not necessary truths, for they could easily be otherwise. On the other hand, what experiments could one conduct, what measurements could one make to prove them? They are the sort of propositions that cannot be conclusively proved and that, therefore, remain open to debate. They are judgements - historical, legal or political. In many, perhaps in most, human activities we have to make judgements about things that we can neither prove nor disprove; we have to make judgements because we have to act - often with serious consequences. Are we going to sentence these four people to long periods of imprisonment? Are we going to risk our lives in the streets of Beijing or Bucharest? It behoves us, therefore, before we make judgements to consider what may be said for and what against them. One definition of 'evidence' in the *Shorter Oxford English Dictionary* is 'Ground for belief; that which tends to prove or disprove any conclusion.' So before we make a judgement we need to consider all that tends to prove or disprove it, all that leads to belief or disbelief. I emphasise *'tends* to prove', for such judgements are not susceptible of absolute proof.

The Place of Evidence

Mostly we use evidence in simple everyday affairs: the absence of Mother's coat and basket from the lobby we take as evidence that she has gone shopping; mud on the carpet is evidence that the children are home from school. The mud is evident and the presence of the children is implied by it. In other words, that which is evident supplies evidence for that which is not evident. More serious and sophisticated reasonings from evidence are made by lawyers and detectives. In the typical detective story the fact that the library where the dead baronet was found had been locked on the inside is taken by the local police as evidence that the dead man had committed suicide. However, the detective hero is not convinced. He searches for other evidence which points even more convincingly the other way - that is, to murder. Having by means of this further evidence made a strong case that the butler did it, he confronts the guilty man towards the end of the story, and the wretch finally confesses. Doubtless the author fears that his readers, and perhaps even the jury, would be uneasy about condemning a man on no more than the greater weight of evidence for murder than that for suicide. A confession removes this unease. However, the case of the Guildford Four (in number 7) reminds us that in real life confessions cannot always be relied on.

Now let us turn to the remaining proposition, number 6, which is an historical proposition. Like numbers 7 and 8, and unlike the rest, it cannot be established solely by reason, nor by experiment, nor by observation. It is a judgement, or rather it is two judgements: that Elizabeth was the last Tudor monarch and that she desired the death of Mary. Now many people would say that the first is a fact, and that only the second is debatable and therefore in need of justification by evidence. But this is not so. That she was the last Tudor monarch is neither 'obvious to the sight' nor 'clear to the understanding' - as the *Shorter Oxford* defines 'evident'. Therefore it needs evidence - in this case historical evidence - to support it. Of course, very few would dispute it, any more than people would dispute number 4. But both are contingent, not necessary, truths and therefore have to be established by evidence. Just how one sets about doing that is a matter for a chemist or an historian. How a chemist uses evidence is not here our concern, and how a historian does we shall look at later.

The Particular Problem of Historical Evidence

Before that we shall note one or two things about history that should not be overlooked. The first thing to notice is that all historical knowledge is indirect knowledge. It is never self-evident (like Propositions 2 and 10 on page 145). Nor does historical knowledge consist of necessary truths that can be arrived at solely by the use of reason - as is the case with numbers 1 and 3. Of course such things were true in the past, as they will be true in the future, for mathematics and logic are unaffected by time. But historical propositions are *about* the past. And we must go further. Most contingent (i.e. non-necessary) truths are said to be empirical: that is, they can be verified by experience as in numbers 4, 5 or 10. But statements about the past are like statements about the centre of the Earth or a remote star. They are beyond the reach of direct experience and have to be established indirectly, if at all. Yet it is not inconceivable that one day men might be about to penetrate to the Earth's centre or even to a distant star. But it is quite impossible to return to the past to verify historical statements by direct experience. Thus we can assert that all knowledge about the past must rest entirely on present evidence. And we can have no more evidence for the past than what is now in existence; though it may not all be known. (In this connection an interesting problem is raised by memory, which is the most familiar form of evidence. For tomorrow I may remember something about yesterday that I cannot recall today. Can I argue that this evidence for yesterday is at this moment in existence? I think so, on the ground that many things are buried in our memories of which we are not always - or even often - conscious. The alternative is to suppose that tomorrow's memory of yesterday will be a new creation, which seems very odd.)

If it seems disappointingly restrictive to realise that all our evidence for the past can be no more than what now exists, we may be encouraged by considering the other side of the coin. This is that every single thing that is now in existence can be taken as evidence for the past. Much of the most interesting progress in the historical profession has been learning how to use previously neglected kinds of evidence - field marks, place names, hedgerows, blood groups, for example. Not only memories, but ideas, beliefs, habits of speech or gesture can all, when rightly interpreted, throw more light on the past. Every working historian is hungry for more evidence, but it is certain that, although exactly what he wants may not be available, there remain quantities of riches yet to be explored.

Common Assumptions about History Challenged

I have spoken both of facts and of interpretation, and it is time to challenge a few common assumptions about history. Among such assumptions are the following:

    a that there exists a core of hard facts, around which
      historians weave various interpretations;

    b that we can have perfectly certain knowledge of some of
      the past;

    c that some evidence can be logically watertight;

d that evidence is independent of judgement; and

e that in areas of uncertainty one person's judgement is as valid as another's.

What I have said may suggest why I believe each of these statements to be untrue. As to (a), it is clear that interpretations (for example, the causes and nature of the French Revolution of 1789 or the Eastern European revolutions of 1989) must rest on a careful consideration of the available evidence. But this also applies to the so-called facts. None are or can be obvious to the sight or the understanding. Even the most undisputed items of historical knowledge (such as that Wellington won the battle of Waterloo in 1815) are indirect knowledge and have to rest on the support of evidence. The difference between a fact and an interpretation in history is that the one is better supported by evidence and commands a wider concurrence of learned agreement than the other. For these reasons it is obvious that assumption (b) is also untenable. As to (c), it follows from what I have said about everything being potentially evidence for the past that we probably do not command all the evidence that may be relevant to any particular issue. Of this yet-to-be-discovered evidence much may support our present conclusion, but it is by no means inconceivable that some new evidence may tell against our current beliefs. Hence in history, as in law, a case can never be proved beyond all possible doubt, but at best decided on a balance of probabilities, however unequal. A law court must be satisfied with a verdict 'beyond all reasonable doubt'. In history we often cannot go even as far as that. In response to (d) and (e) I believe that the concept of evidence necessarily involves that of judgement, and that some people are better qualified than others to make judgements. Let me enlarge on these points.

Evidence and Evaluation

We have seen that evidence is relevant to areas of uncertainty. We do not need evidence either for that which is directly evident (as in numbers 2, 9 and 10 on page 145) or for what is necessarily, if not obviously, true (as in number 3). In other cases we use what is evident as evidence for what is not evident - as footprints in the Himalayan snows have been taken as evidence for the Abominable

Snowman or fingerprints on a knife as evidence for the identification of the murderer. But even after evidence has been adduced it usually happens that the case is not regarded as closed beyond all doubt; there is contrary evidence to be considered: in these examples, no man-sized anthropoid is known outside tropical Africa, or the accused may have a sound alibi. In short, one item of evidence may point to a certain conclusion (the Snowman or the murderer), but the connection is not conclusive. In addition there may well be contrary evidence. Thus questions of fact (as distinct from questions of logic or mathematics) have properly to be settled by due consideration of a number or items of (sometimes conflicting) evidence. The words 'settled' and 'consideration' in the previous sentence remind us that arguing from the seen to the unseen like this calls for sound judgement. Now judgement is an activity of rational minds, but (unlike mathematics) it does not lead necessarily and inexorably to one conclusion. Art, religion and politics are important spheres of human activity where the best minds, faced with the same evidence, may come rationally and responsibly to quite different conclusions. That this should also happen (though less frequently) in law, history and science should not surprise us.

The question now arises: Who are the 'best minds' to assess the relevant evidence and draw the proper conclusion? The answer surely is: The recognised experts in that field. To determine whether a painting is a Titian or a Giorgione we turn to an art historian; to decide which way the stag or the lion went we ask the gillie or the hunter; in a criminal case the court may consult scientists about bloodstains or bullet trajectories, and so on. But in questions of general human behaviour it is a jury of twelve ordinary citizens, whose very ordinariness makes them the relevant experts to decide upon guilt or innocence - or, more precisely in English law, to decide whether the prosecution has established its case beyond all reasonable doubt. To sum up, it is not sufficient to say that A is evidence of B, but that *in the judgement of a person P* A is evidence of B; more shortly, A is evidence *of* B *for* P. Thus, 'being evidence' is not a two-term but a three-term relation.

Having considered evidence in general, we may now turn to historical evidence in particular and to some of the problems it poses for the working historian. For it is now clear that the historian does not work through logic (like a mathematician), nor by empirical method, that is, observation and experiment (like a natural scientist), nor by assembling indisputable 'facts' as a naturalist might collect butterflies or birds' eggs. (Few people nowadays would accept this last as a description of how a historian works, though it was put forward with some authority by J.B. Bury in his Inaugural Lecture as Regius Professor of Modern History at Cambridge in 1902 when he spoke of 'the faith that a complete assemblage of the smallest facts of human history will tell in the end.' To be fair, Bury goes on to say that 'it does not follow that we should confine ourselves to the collection and classification of materials . . .' The whole lecture is still worth reading.) On the contrary, the historian does his work by a series of fallible judgements based on all the available evidence. He does his best to arrive at sound conclusions, but he is always aware that in some cases no firm conclusion can (yet) be reached, and in others that his position may well be overthrown either by the appearance of more evidence than he has used or by a fresh consideration of his evidence. That is why the prudent historian neglects no relevant evidence, whether it tells for or against his conclusion. Nevertheless, the firmest positions in historiography are not beyond assault.

Evidence used in the Reconstruction of the Past

What sort of judgements then does the student of history have to make about his evidence? (Perhaps here I should explain that it is only for reasons of brevity that I use the masculine pronouns. I owe much to women historians, and if anyone in reading this cares to substitute 'she' and 'her' for 'he', 'him' and 'his' I have no objection.) First, he should be aware that the use of historical evidence calls for both 'vertical' and 'horizontal' knowledge, or, more accurately, diachronic and synchronic knowledge; for he has to consider things that happen one after the other and things that happen simultaneously. Let me explain.

In order to learn about an occurrence or a state of affairs in the past, one has to start with present evidence and then, from there, move backwards in time. Thus, before claiming any knowledge about what happened in the past, one has to be fairly sure of two things: that one knows what the present evidence actually is, not what at first sight it appears to be, and then that one can accurately reconstruct (backwards as it were) the process that links the past to the present. Let me offer a personal example. Once I remarked to a student of mine that his native town ought at some time to have had a castle. He agreed, but said that no one had ever heard of one. I suggested that he examine the older buildings in this small town to see whether they incorporated any large, worked stones incongruous with the small stones, bricks or timber of which the houses were mostly built. He agreed to look for such and to plot them on a sheet of transparent paper laid over a large-scale ordnance map. Some weeks later he produced this paper (without the map) and asked me to suggest where the castle might have been. It was not difficult to place one's finger on the spot where the marks clustered most thickly. He then produced the map and showed that this spot was the summit of a small hill which would seem the most obvious place to site a castle. (Later he went off to hunt for documentary evidence of a castle, but I never heard whether he succeeded.) The point, however, is clear. If there ever was a castle at the spot we supposed, then it is in accord with what we know happened elsewhere to believe that it was dismantled and the valuable stones were incorporated in lesser but still existing buildings. But the two relevant questions are: were the extant blocks really of worked stone, not shaped by nature or, perhaps, made of concrete? And, secondly, did they come from an earlier castle or other great building? We had to be right about both what the evidence actually *is*, and by what processes it came to be where it is now found. This is what I mean by 'vertical knowledge' - a knowledge of how present evidence is likely to be linked, over a stretch of time, with a past occurrence or state of affairs.

Now for 'horizontal knowledge'. Walking in the country we may find that the plough has turned up a quantity of what appear to be musket balls, rusty swords, spearheads, buckles, etc. These never constituted a battle, which consisted of large bodies of men, filled with varying emotions of determination, hatred, loyalty or fear, engaged in slaughtering each other, or, at least, in not being slaughtered and so abandoning their equipment as they ran away. These pathetic scraps of metal were only a small part of what had been a phenomenon of blood, noise, smoke, flame, terror and death. But they very suggestively point to the events that occurred at the same time that they were scattered on the ground. To be able, in our imagination, to connect the two requires 'horizontal knowledge' - knowledge of how the things that have remained were once connected with simultaneously existing things that have not remained. Lest this sort of reconstruction seem too easy to be worth discussing, let us remember how often archaeologists come across an object (the notorious *'bâton de commandement'*, for example) or historians a document (e.g. an unsigned and undated letter) whose function is far from clear and which presents a real problem in placing it in its proper context.

These are some of the more important problems, logical and epistemological, that relate to the use of evidence in general. A consideration of the sorts of evidence that historians use and the various ways that they use them would require more space than is now at my disposal, but I should like to think that what I have said is of some help towards a deeper understanding of what is involved in good historical work.

Evidence and the Historian (II)

Faith, St. Paul wrote to the Hebrews, is evidence for things not seen. In these days, when we are told that history in schools must contain more facts, it is salutary to remember that, strictly speaking, the historian has no facts, only evidence - that is, if by 'facts' we mean statements that are certainly true. Of course, many historical statements (for example, statements of the deaths of kings and queens) are accepted as true because the evidence for them is overwhelming. Nevertheless, any statement about the past is a statement about 'things not seen'. Thus it rests on nothing more than conclusions more or less reliably drawn from evidence. As I said in my previous article, 'that which is evident supplies evidence for that which is not evident'. All historical knowledge consists of conclusions *about the past* drawn from evidence *in the present*. And, as with St. Paul, the acceptance of these conclusions requires an element of faith.

All this, however, does not mean that we should be as sceptical as Catherine Morland in *Northanger Abbey*. This young lady said of history, 'I often think it odd that it should be so dull, for a great deal of it must be invention'. (Indeed, without the fictive element most history would be a great deal duller, but that is another story.) In practice the big question is: How much faith should we put in what the historian tells us? Partly the answer is that we should 'listen out for the buzzing' (of the bees in the historian's bonnet) - as E.H. Carr advises us. But this advice takes us only so far; it warns of bias, but it does not help us to sort out the true from the false, or, rather the more from the less probable. To do this we need to look at the material on which the historian has built; that is, we need to know what evidence the historian has used (and not used) and how she has used it.

What follows is divided into three sections, A, B and C, which need not, however, be read only in that order.

A. How the Historian Works

It may seem presumptuous to attempt to describe how 'the' historian works, for histories of countless topics have been written in many different ways in every civilised nation by men and women of widely varying degrees of ability for over 2000 years. How can one hope to identify 'the' historian? Nevertheless, it is possible to distinguish five stages of the work that most good histories have gone through. (It must be emphasised that these stages are not always followed through in this order, and there will always have been many shifts back and forth between the stages.)

First, the historian looks for a subject. Sometimes, as in the cases of Herodotus, Thucydides, Joinville, Froissart, Clarendon, Trotsky, Churchill, the historian feels compelled to record and explain the great events in which he himself played a part. The armchair scholar, on the other hand, may choose whatever subject appeals. Gibbon was determined to be a historian long before he hit on the decline and fall of Rome. First he examined and rejected such varied topics as the Italian expedition of Charles VIII, a comparison of Henry V with the Emperor Titus, and a life of Sir Walter Raleigh. He tells us in his autobiography: 'It was at Rome, on the 15th of October 1764, as I sat musing amidst the ruins of the Capitol, while the barefooted friars were singing vespers in the temple of Jupiter, that the idea of writing the decline and fall of the city first started to my mind.' That was the birth of the greatest historical work in the English language.

Second, the historian seeks out, evaluates, selects and, perhaps, prepares the evidence to be used. (This will be discussed in more detail later.)

Third, he or she will attentively study (reading and digesting as they go) all the available sources. In the next section we look at what these may be. Here it is important to note that this study goes hand in hand with the next stage as they move back and forth between them. This is largely because judgements of relevance (of how useful or important certain evidence may be) change as the work goes on.

Fourth, from their study of the evidence - primary and secondary sources of all kinds - the historians will be building up in their mind a mental picture of just how things were in the past. As this picture achieves greater definition (perhaps not only in their minds, but now also on paper), they will be led to further pieces of evidence and often to a re-examination and re-consideration of evidence already used. It is this that E.H. Carr describes as 'a continuous process of interaction between a historian and his facts'. (He should more properly have spoken of evidence, not facts.)

Fifth, but not necessarily finally, comes the casting of their mental picture (made up of many evidential judgements) into coherent form. Leaving aside such visual representations of the past as paintings, pageants, plays, operas and films, we may say that this coherent form is generally a verbal structure (book, article, lecture) that purports to represent something of the past. As such it is a work of art and must be subject to all the onslaughts of literary criticism - involving questions of genre, mode, trope, text and context, authority, intentionality, discourse, etc, but these are by no means our concern here.

B. What the Historian Uses

Turning now to the evidence that the historian may use, we consider in turn primary and secondary evidence, types of evidence, hard and soft evidence, and intentional and non-intentional evidence.

1 PRIMARY AND SECONDARY SOURCES. A primary source is a piece of evidence whose origin is contemporary with the period in question - thus the Domesday Book for the Norman Conquest (though not the battle of Hastings), or Wellington's despatches for the Peninsular War. A secondary source is a study, usually by a historian, of the period under review, or some aspect of it. This is written after (often long after) the period. All reputable historical research must be based on primary sources. Work in the archives is

as essential to the historian as laboratory work to the scientist. Scientists do not spend all their time in the lab., nor historians in the archives, but the experience acquired there is essential to both professions, and their conclusions must be open to verification in both places. At the end of their books scholars distinguish between primary and secondary sources used.

To appreciate why this distinction is made we may recall the case (familiar to Dickens' lovers) of Bardell v. Pickwick, recorded in *The Pickwick Papers,* chapter xxxiv. To Sam Weller's jocular and irrelevant remarks ('. . . as the soldier said when . . .') the judge thunders: 'You must not tell us what the soldier, or any other man, said, sir. It isn't evidence.' Evidence in a court of law must be at first-hand; hence the summoning of witnesses and the production of exhibits. For a similar reason historians in their quest of the truth prefer to go to the raw material before it has been processed in any way by someone else's ideas.

However, this is not to say that secondary sources can be ignored. Historians, it is generally agreed, should not venture to set pen to paper until they have read widely and deeply (if not exhaustively) in what others have had to say on the subject. Indeed, they can hardly get their bearings at all or find out what questions are to be asked until they have read their predecessors. Nevertheless, there are difficulties. In an interesting essay (see *Man On His Past,* chapter v) Herbert Butterfield illustrates how historians over decades can be misled by an accepted but erroneous version of events. (One recalls A.J.P. Taylor's remark that history does not repeat itself - historians repeat each other.) 'The old story has dug itself deep and made grooves in our minds,' writes Butterfield. For centuries historians were blind, as he shows, to the importance of Russia's role in the outbreak of the Seven Years' War in 1756. 'It is easy', he says, 'to think that we are being faithful and merely transcribing the evidence when unconsciously we are running the evidence into an ancient mould'. To the study of secondary sources we may apply Pope's advice:

> A little learning is a dang'rous thing;
> Drink deep or taste not the Pierian spring:
> There shallow draughts intoxicate the brain,
> And drinking largely sobers us again.

Primary and secondary sources cannot always be easily distinguished, however. We observed that two things characterise primary material: that it is contemporary and that it is unprocessed. If, as is commonly done, we use the first criterion alone to distinguish primary from secondary, then problems arise in relation to the other one.

To begin with, what of the editions of printed documents? A large proportion of the relevant papers for medieval and early modern history have been collected, transcribed, ordered and published. This is a great convenience for the historian, who would otherwise not be able to consult more than a fraction of these materials. An easy way to gain some idea of how much has been done in this respect is to consult the bibliographies at the back of the earlier volumes of the *Oxford History of England*. A visit to a university or large reference library will show these volumes (Calendars of Close Rolls, Letters and Papers of Henry VIII, State Papers Domestic, State Papers Venetian, etc.) marching side by side for scores of yards of shelving. There are drawbacks, however. One is that the very quantity conceals the fact that not all the relevant documents may be there. Moreover, some of them are only partially transcribed. Also there is the possibility that errors have crept into the transcription or the printing. And finally the historian is denied the clues that the original document may afford by way of ink, handwriting, paper or vellum, format, etc. Nevertheless, the printing of sources is invaluable. This becomes even more apparent in European history. Four well-known histories in paperback will illustrate the point: Steven Runciman's *History of the Crusades;* Geoffrey Parker's *The Dutch Revolt* - a book whose bibliography contains particularly interesting discussions of evidence; R.J.W. Evans' *The Making of the Habsburg Monarchy;* and J.H. Elliott's *The Count-Duke of Olivares.* These authors have each read source materials in five, six or more languages, including Czech and Hungarian (Evans), Greek (Runciman) and Dutch (Parker). A facility in French, German, Italian, Spanish and Latin is common to them all - probably as a matter of course. Although they have studied some original documents, most of their work must have been based on printed sources (as their bibliographies indicate), because the twin difficulties of gaining access to distant repositories and of deciphering a foreign language in a foreign hand would have been too costly in time and labour. The point here is that, necessary as they are, such printed sources cannot be considered completely unprocessed raw material.

A second problem arises with pamphlets (from the sixteenth century on) and with newspapers (from the seventeenth century on). These, being strictly contemporary, show what at least some people at the time thought of the events in question. As such they are good primary sources. But when you consider how ill-informed, biased and even unscrupulous the writers and printers are likely to have been, you realise that they are not good evidence for the events themselves. In this respect, newspapers and pamphlets are far from being unprocessed raw material.

Then there are contemporary chronicles and histories. This is not the place to discuss the three basic types of historical representation - annals, the chronicle, and the history proper. Enough here to note that such works (even the apparently simple *Anglo-Saxon Chronicle*) at least provide a skeleton chronology for ordering events in time. Some venture upon cause and explanation. The more informed discuss motive and the interplay of personality. The more educated (profiting from the humanism of the Italian Renaissance) consciously model themselves upon classical authors and attempt to write political or 'philosophical' histories - for example, Machiavelli and Guicciardini in Florence, Polydore Vergil and Thomas More in England, Philippe de Commynes in France. In an appendix to his *Edward IV* Charles Ross laments the lack of such contemporary historians for that reign, and he quotes G.R. Elton: 'It is because no sound contemporary history exists for this age that its shape and meaning are so much in dispute now' (p. 429).

And what are we to make of those histories written while the events recounted are still in train? Geoffrey Parker records thirty-four contemporary histories of the revolt of the Netherlands. (See his *The Dutch Revolt*, p. 277.) We may also call to mind that several books have already (1990) been published on Mrs Thatcher and her governments while still in power. Before we dismiss all these as too premature to be worth serious consideration - for they must be lacking both in essential information and in the perspective given by distance, we should remember that one of the acknow-ledged masterpieces of the historian's art, Thucydides' *History of the Peloponnesian War*, is just such a 'premature' effort. Contemporary, yes. But unprocessed raw material? Hardly. Yet it is almost all we have to go on for our knowledge of that great conflict.

Finally, and most problematic of all, is the evidence of the imaginative literature of an age. It is easy to sneer at the facile attempts, fashionable in the first half of this century to write social histories of The World of Chaucer, The England of Shakespeare or The London of Dickens based largely upon supposed facts drawn from the poetry, plays and novels of these writers. (Arthur Marwick, in *The Nature of History*, p. 139, gives a good example of how such misconceived histories have been led astray.) These fictions supply no hard evidence; yet it is difficult to believe that one could have as deep an insight into the England of Edward III, Elizabeth I or Victoria if Chaucer, Shakespeare and Dickens had never written. Such writers supply contemporary evidence without a doubt, but it is difficult to state precisely evidence for what.

2 TYPES OF EVIDENCE. In a famous attempt about a hundred years ago to make history a more scientific discipline, two French scholars, C.V. Langlois and C. Seignobos, wrote an *Introduction to the Study of History* in which they ruled that history essentially depended on documentary evidence - 'no documents, no history'. If this was an attempt to rule out other sources of history (for example, architecture, art and archaeology, of which historians had long been making use) it was a spectacular failure. Within a few years the American James Harvey Robinson opened his *The New History* thus: 'In its amplest meaning History includes every trace and vestige of everything that man has done or thought since first he appeared on the earth . . . Its sources of information extend from the rude flint hatchets of Chelles to this morning's newspaper.' One of the most remarkable characteristics of twentieth-century historiography is that historians have found an ever-widening range of material to furnish evidence of the past - not only the flints and potsherds of the archaeologist, but crop patterns, hedgerows, ruined and rejected machinery, folk-songs, myths, memories, blood-groups, parish registers, land surveys, account books, place-names, sunken wrecks and much more. It seems that now all is grist that comes to the historian's mill. The truth is that anything whatever (whether material or ideal) that remains from the past (however remote, however recent) furnishes some evidence for that past. What is required is the ability to read that evidence aright.

3 HARD AND SOFT EVIDENCE. One important element in this explosion of historical sources is statistical evidence. While some kinds of evidence are fairly sparse (for example, for ancient Greek cities other than Athens or eleventh-century charters) other kinds are voluminous - for example, the births, deaths and marriages

recorded in thousands of parishes in this and other countries. From these has arisen a whole new science of historical demography: that is, the statistical study of populations in the past. A good short introduction to this important subject is E.A. Wrigley's *Population and History*, which is based on the larger work under Wrigley's editorship, *An Introduction to English Historical Demography*. Of great value to historians of England is the massive work that he produced with R.S. Schofield, *The Population History of England 1541-1871: A Reconstruction*. The pioneer work in this field was, of course, Thomas Malthus's *First Essay on Population*, but a full development of the theory had to wait until A. Sauvy's *Théorie générale de la population*.

Two modern advances have made possible the extension of historical research into areas where vast amounts of data present hitherto insoluble problems: these are the development of statistical theory and the invention of the micro-chip leading to ever more powerful computers. Economic historians have thus been able to measure populations, land-holdings, imports and exports, rents, profits, exchange rates, yields of fields and mines, profitability, investment and economic growth. Two useful introductions to quantitative history are Michael Drake (ed.), *Applied Historical Studies* and Roderick Floud (ed.), *Essays in Quantitative History*, especially the cautionary essay in the latter by G. Ohlin, 'No Safety in Numbers: Some Pitfalls of Historical Statistics'. A French approach to quantitative history is found in the work of the *Annales* school of historians, of which a good example is E. Le Roy Ladurie, *The Territory of the Historian*. Such historical evidence, processed by statistics and embodied in computer print-outs, is expressed in numbers and symbols rather than words and sentences. Such measurements carry great authority in the eyes of econometric and 'cliometric' historians. This is known as 'hard' evidence.

By contrast, 'soft' evidence is found in more conventional historical documents, where it is couched in words not figures, and where it often expresses ideas rather than quantities. (Think, for example, of political and constitutional documents - Magna Carta, the Act in Restraint of Appeals of 1533 or the American Declaration of Independence.) The epithet 'soft' suggests that the material is disputable, qualifiable, even malleable. It is open to more than one interpretation; people argue endlessly about what exactly it means. 'Not so with our hard evidence', boast the cliometricians. 'Ours is quantifiable and unambiguous.' But not everything is quantifiable.

For example, sociologists insist that our social reality consists of beliefs, conventions, customs, institutions - which boil down to ideas. But how do you write the history of ideas? Many people try, but, as one political historian said, that is like nailing jelly to the wall. R.G. Collingwood has famously argued that history can only be the history of thought. Material objects are not self-explanatory. Their meanings are not borne on their faces - not even coins or monuments - if we cannot read the language or reconstruct the social conventions, as many a baffled archaeologist has discovered. Because soft evidence is in words, not numbers, there arise all the problems of language - of translation, of intention, of comprehension. Notoriously, one can never be sure that a string of words means the same to the hearer or reader as to the speaker or writer - or even to another hearer or reader. With numbers there is little doubt. There is less ambiguity in '10' or '365' than in words like 'crown' or 'Vaterland'. But we must still ask in the former case, What has been counted? How correctly? And by whom? When? and Where?

There is not space here to argue the respective merits and demerits of hard and soft evidence. The intelligent reader can think of some of them for herself. The working historian has to use both kinds, if possible, and know how to evaluate them for her purposes.

4 INTENTIONAL AND NON-INTENTIONAL EVIDENCE. The last distinction to be made is between evidence which is intended for the eyes of some future enquirer and that which is not so intended. Marc Bloch in his sadly uncompleted work, *The Historian's Craft* makes the distinction admirably clear. When we read histories or memoirs or battle reports, 'we are only doing exactly what the writers expected us to do'. But the prehistoric woman who threw her garbage into a lake or river, the medieval businessman who wrote-up his accounts had not 'the least desire to influence the opinions of contemporaries or of future historians' (pp. 60-62). Although the historian cannot do without evidence of the first kind, she is rightly distrustful of it - as if she were buying a second-hand car or a middle-aged horse. Evidence of the second kind has no intention to mislead her, but it presents problems of understanding. It does not come out to meet her, as it were. What exactly is meant by this sentence in a politician's letter? What was the function of this peculiar piece of metal or that hole in the wall? Some of these problems will be discussed in the next section.

C. Some Problems of the Material

We have looked at how the historian works and at the sort of evidence on which her work is based. Now we glance briefly at a few of the difficulties that can arise in the use of that evidence. They may be considered under the seven headings of Provenance, Access, Language, Reliability, Context, Interpretation and Relevance. Much could be said on each. Here it is possible to indicate only a few of the problems.

1 Provenance. One of the most important questions to be asked of any document or other artefact is the same as that which art dealers always ask about a painting: Through whose hands has this passed? It is by no means always obvious where and when the document originated, nor why it was produced. I have often had in my hands documents almost certainly written at a time and place other than that stated therein. Indeed, it is often hard to tell copies from originals. Nor is it always easy to detect what may have been added to or deleted from them. Since the establishment of public archives, documents are rarely still in their place of origin. Even then they may have been removed and returned. No artefact, whether written document or chipped flint, bears its meaning and purpose on its face.

2 Access. Most documents that a historian is likely to need are now collected in public repositories - libraries, record offices etc. In spite of the courteous help usually provided by the custodians, researchers face difficulties in actually getting at the documents. There are restrictions of number (only a certain number of readers can be accommodated at once), of time (short opening hours, and closure in the evenings, at weekends and public holidays - just the times when many researchers are free for the work), of secrecy (British government records are subject to a thirty-year delay and after that are likely to have been 'weeded' of many valuable papers), and of distance (for all but Londoners the Public Record Office at Kew is a long way off, and for some British records one may nowadays have to go to New England, Texas or California. Foreign policy studies or European history can mean journeys to several Continental cities). For all these reasons, to go back for a second look as the work advances and new doubts and questions arise is often impracticable. Frustration!

3 Language. English history before the seventeenth century calls for some knowledge of Latin and before the fourteenth century of medieval French also. For foreign relations and European history a number of other languages are needed, as we have seen in Section B previously. Asian or African history presents no less of a problem. How can a historian, struggling to master half a dozen foreign languages, grasp the subtleties and nuances of each? (Every schoolboy knows of the historian who asserted that Catherine of Aragon was devoted to her nephew, Charles V, because she ended each letter, 'I kiss your hand'. He did not realise that the phrase was, to a sixteenth-century Spaniard, as meaningless as 'Yours sincerely'.) One solution is to rely on documents already translated. But translations are not beyond dispute, as Marwick shows in his remarks on the Anglo-Saxon Chronicle in *The Nature of History*, p. 138. And apart from questions of accuracy, what of the documents not already translated?

4 Reliability. Having found some more or less satisfactory answers to all these problems, the historian then has to question the author of the document before her. Whether he is reporting a riot or recording a cargo of wine, the writer has his own purposes and intentions: is he exaggerating or underplaying the commotion? Is he stating exactly how much wine came in? Even if the writer is trying to be scrupulously truthful, was he in a position to know the facts? Did he see the beginning of the riot and survey every street simultaneously? Was he actually on the quayside in the rain when the wine was unloaded and did he then search the ship? Finally, we may ask whether the twentieth-century reader fully grasps the meaning of words written centuries earlier. This leads on to:

5 Context. Whether we are considering written statements or recorded actions, we are compelled to ask about meaning. What did he or she or they intend by writing or speaking or acting like this? What would contemporaries understand by it? Such questions can be only answered in terms of a wider knowledge of that world, of the socio-politico-economic setting in which the actions took place. As any literature student knows, texts have to be read in context. And, for the historian, not only texts, but words and actions too. And this includes knowing also the 'vertical' context - i.e. the preceding and succeeding events.

6 Interpretation. Only after all this can the researcher be confident that she has properly understood what was done, said or written at the time and place under review - perhaps the Rome of the Caesars or perhaps the Germany of Adolf Hitler. Not only must the documents be construed; the whole course of events has to be interpreted and a meaning assigned to it. And very often some extension of the context - to embrace a wider field, a later or earlier series of events, or a different point of view - will alter the interpretation. We must remind ourselves that even the most confident of historical assertions are no more than interpretations of evidence.

7 Relevance. In excitement at a new discovery, a series of very legible documents, or in fascination with an intriguing tale, the historian may be led astray from her strict purpose. It is a weakness of all but the most disciplined of historians to recount what seems important, amusing, interesting, salacious or exciting, but which is not strictly relevant to the matter in hand. How often in reading history does one want to say to the author, 'Yes, but what is the point of telling me this?' Historians should never cease to question themselves: 'Have I ignored nothing that is relevant? Have I included anything that is irrelevant?'

In conclusion I should like to emphasise two things. One is that all these problems and difficulties render it useless for anyone to be dogmatic about the facts, the meaning, or even the proper methods of history. The other is that it is the challenge of these same problems and the varied intellectual efforts they call for that make historical research so stimulating, so rewarding and, often, such sheer fun. One is, after all, getting close to those real men and women of the past in the only way possible. It is no wonder that many people find historical research so enthralling.

Books consulted (the place of publication can be assumed to be London unless stated otherwise). Marc Bloch, *The Historian's Craft,* Manchester, 1954 (English edn.). Herbert Butterfield, *Man on His Past,* Cambridge, 1955. E.H. Carr, *What is History?* 1961. G. Kitson Clark, *The Critical Historian,* 1967. R.G. Collingwood, *The Idea of History,* Oxford, 1946. Arthur Marwick, *The Nature of History,* 1970. Michael Stanford, *The Nature of Historical Knowledge,* Oxford, 1986. Haydon White, *The Content of the Form,* Baltimore, 1987.

Dr Michael Stanford is author of *The Nature of Historical Knowledge,* Oxford, 1986.

Dialogues with Documents

a The English Civil War

AMONG THE QUALITIES which historians most seek in their source material are a date contemporary to the events to which it refers, detailed and precise information, and an easy and convincing assimilation into what is known already of its context. All these requirements are met by two pamphlets published in London towards the end of 1642. Both refer to military events in the Severn and Wye valleys in the early stages of the Great Civil War. The King had occupied Oxford and was advancing upon London with his main field army. South Wales was being secured for his cause by the Marquis of Hertford and, under his command, Lord Herbert. Between these two blocs of royalist territory lay parliamentarian garrisons at Gloucester, Worcester and Hereford commanded by the Earl of Stamford, who was based in the last of those towns. The pamphlets concerned describe attempts by Hertford and Herbert to defeat the Earl and to close the gap between them and the royalist Midlands.

The first, *True Newes out of Herefordshire*, was published in London by Francis Wright, shortly before 19 November when it was collected by a bookseller. It described how Hertford and Herbert had mustered 7000 men near Cardiff upon the 4th, and marched on Hereford. Finding it strongly fortified, they moved south-east into Gloucestershire. Stamford mustered his own regiment and called up the local militia to give himself an army of 4000 soldiers. With this he faced the royalists near Tewkesbury on the 15th. Their two noble commanders led a cavalry charge which was held by Stamford's pikemen. Then Hertford's brother Lord Seymour led up the infantry, but they were raw levies with bad equipment while Stamford had well-trained men, good muskets and field artillery. When Seymour's horse was killed under him and Colonel Sir Rhys ap Huw Granock was shot down, the Welsh fled and suffered fearful losses. Some 2500 were buried in pits and 1200 led away prisoner, while the Earl lost only 160 dead. Now, the description and the location of the battle are all plausible, and so are the relative casualty figures, given the difference in quality of the two forces. All the individuals named are known to history except Sir Rhys, and he also is a credible personality, given that our records for the Welsh gentry and royalist armies of the time are very imperfect.

The second tract, *A True Relation of a Most blessed Victory*, was published in London on 3 December by L. Wright, which may be a misprint for the F. Wright who produced the first one. It describes how, on 27 November, Hertford had once again advanced upon Hereford with thousands of men, hearing that Stamford's force inside was reduced to only 1500 soldiers. The Earl put a party in ambush near a ford, and then drew up the rest outside the town with a speech about the justice of their cause. When the royalists attacked, the parliamentarian force divided, wheeling to left and right to reveal three cannon which fired into the Welsh at close range, followed by musketry. This held up Hertford's army until Stamford's was reinforced heavily by local people rallying to it with their weapons. The royalists then retired, only to be taken in the rear by the ambush and broken into headlong flight. Hertford lost another 2000 men and only survived himself by hiding in a wood. The circumstantial detail in this account is much less vivid than in the first one, and the manoeuvre to expose the cannon sounds a little farfetched. But with veterans, in the face of raw recruits, it would be possible, and the precision of the dating, the place and the protagonists is again impressive.

All this would explain why, from the time of J.R. Phillips's classic study of the Civil War in Wales and the Marches, published in 1874, these two narratives have been accepted as fact. Historians up to and including Joyce Malcolm, in 1983, have used them as evidence both for the relative popularity of the two causes and for a massive attrition of royalist strength in South Wales which may have helped to avert a victory for the King in late 1642. All these writers might have done well to heed a local historian of Herefordshire, the Reverend John Webb, who worked earlier in the nineteenth century than Phillips. He dismissed the two tracts in a sentence, for he had noticed a different and much better source for their subject. This consisted of Stamford's own reports back to Parliament, which were entered in the journals of the House of Lords. One was written on 16 November, the day after he is supposed to have won his great victory at Tewkesbury. It does not mention the entire campaign, but describes instead a raid upon a few companies of royalists quartered in a village eight miles from Hereford. These were routed with the loss of 21 men, but the Earl had cause to complain of the hostility of the local people which made intelligence hard to gather. In another letter from Hereford dated 3 December, six days after his second battle is supposed to have been won outside the town, he describes no recent operations at all. Instead he complains again of the hatred of the surrounding population and of his lack of money and supplies. The royalists had fortified a post only five miles away, and he feared that his position was becoming untenable. So indeed it proved, for soon after he retreated from the county and left it to the enemy.

The inescapable conclusion is that both pamphlets are packs of lies, concocted deliberately to deceive the Londoners. With the King advancing on the capital, somebody had the idea of spinning tales of royalist defeats in his rear, to make Parliament's cause appear still vital and viable. Hence the glorious and gory battles, the fictitious speech by Stamford to inspire his troops, and the accounts of the ability of the Earl to rally the local militia and countryfolk to his cause. The latter gave an impression of the popularity of Parliament's cause on the Welsh border utterly at variance with the truth. In the process the unknown author(s) managed to deceive, if not their public, a great many historians. It is a chilling thought that if the Lords had not resolved to record Stamford's despatches then these fraudulent narratives would have become an enduring part of the story of the Civil War and helped to mould our attitude to it. The conclusion that follows is surely that *no* Civil War pamphlet or newspaper, however apparently plausible, can be accepted as historical evidence unless corroborated by completely independent material. In which case a fair amount of what has been written about the war, up to the present moment, must now be undone as it has been based upon such sources. It is a daunting notion that modern historiography has yet to rise to the standards set by a country clergyman over a hundred years ago.   Dr Ronald Hutton.

b Italian Unification

HISTORIANS MUST 'GO BACK TO THE DOCUMENTS', but the documents are not likely to answer our questions straightforwardly. One document on its own hardly ever does so. To decide what reliance to place on a particular document, we have to know who wrote it, when and in what circumstances. Even more background information may be required before we can determine what a document actually means. Gladstone wrote in his diary for Thursday 14 April 1864: 'Went, by a desperate push, to see Garibaldi welcomed at the Opera. It was good, but not like the people.'[1] What does this entry tell the historian?

Gladstone's diaries have come down to us complete, most carefully and securely preserved. There is no doubt whatever that these are Gladstone's own words, written under the immediate impression of the event in which he had just been involved. Moreover, the diary was an absolutely private document, intended to be seen by no one else, at least during his lifetime. He kept it as an account for God of his use of his life and time. So this is a piece of first-hand, untainted, contemporary evidence.

In April 1864, four years after leading the expedition that conquered Sicily and Naples from the Bourbons and made possible the unification of Italy, Giuseppe Garibaldi came to England. On Monday 11 April, when he arrived in London, he received an unparalleled reception from vast and enthusiastic yet peaceful crowds. Gladstone did not mention it in his entry for the 11th. But nearly all the historians who have used his entry of the 14th assume that it means roughly this: 'I went through dense crowds to see Garibaldi welcomed at the Opera (at Covent Garden). The reception given him by these rich people was splendid, but nothing like so striking as the enthusiasm shown by ordinary people.' That sentiment fits in with the usual account of Gladstone's political development. Having started as a right-wing Tory in the 1830s, he became a Free Trader in the forties, a supporter of Italian reform movements in the fifties and a member of a Liberal Cabinet in 1859. He welcomed the creation of a new united Kingdom of Italy in 1861. On speaking tours in the provinces he became intoxicated with the applause of crowds. A month after seeing Garibaldi at the Opera, on

11 May 1864, he was to make a sensational Commons speech on Baines's Bill which was taken by radical leaders to signalise his conversion to parliamentary reform of a democratic tendency. He was already well on the way to becoming a uniquely popular politician, 'the People's William'.

On the other hand, Gladstone had reservations about Italian unification; he played a prominent part in persuading Garibaldi to leave the country unexpectedly early, which meant his abandoning a lengthy planned provincial tour; Gladstone himself denied that his speech on Baines's Bill marked any change in his position; and, whatever his rhetoric, his line in the debates on the Second Reform Act in 1867 was in many ways more conservative than Disraeli's. One historian, impressed by this side of the story, has asserted that the second sentence of Gladstone's diary entry for 14 April really meant: 'the reception at the Opera was a fine sight, but it was not characteristic of the people concerned.'[2] I reject this claim for many reasons. It seems, for example, to depend on suppressing Gladstone's underlining of the word 'people'; and Professor Shannon's biography of Gladstone gives other examples of Gladstone using the phrase 'the people' with evident approval and admiration.[3] But exactly what he meant by it remains hard to determine.

My other extract is completely different in origin. It comes from the Syllabus of Errors, a formal public statement issued by the papacy on 2 December 1864 after years of consideration and consultation. As with my first document, its date and authenticity are in no doubt whatever. I take the most famous of the errors listed, number 80. Translated from Latin, this is what it condemned: 'The Roman Pontiff can and should reconcile himself and reach agreement with progress, Liberalism and recent departures in civil society.'[4] At first glance, to condemn this view is equivalent to condemning 'all progress, Liberalism and recent departures in civil society'. Hence this clause of the Syllabus appalled Protestants and Liberals everywhere, including the important minority of Liberals within the Roman Catholic Church itself. But the Syllabus was not a brand-new document. It was a collection of previous papal statements, some of them dating back many years, republished out of their context. The condemnation of Error 80 came from an 'Allocution' of 1861 denouncing the policy of the new kingdom of Italy towards the papal state and the church, especially in regard to education. The Liberal Bishop Dupanloup argued in a pamphlet published early in 1865 that the Syllabus was only saying that the Pope could not be expected to accept all manifestations of progress, Liberalism etc. The British envoy in Rome told the Pope that he could not reconcile the Syllabus with Dupanloup's pamphlet, but hoped that Dupanloup was right. The Pope replied:

> Tell your Government that Mgr Dupanloup's pamphlet is a beautiful thing . . . and that I have thanked him for it . . . The true meaning of my words I have in my breast. To understand them you must read the original documents. The Principles of the Church are eternal and unchangeable. Circumstances and conditions vary - that liberty of conscience and toleration I condemn here, I claim in England and other foreign countries for the Catholic Church.[5]

A document of undoubted authenticity can be very difficult to interpret. But, before a historian can use it, he has to decide what he thinks it means.

Notes

1 First quoted by J. Morley, *The Life of William Gladstone*, 3 vols, London, 1903, vol. II, p. 111.
2 D.M. Schreuder, 'Gladstone and Italian unification, 1848-70: the making of a Liberal?', *English Historical Review*, LXXXV, 1970, p. 493.
3 R.T. Shannon, *Gladstone*, vol. I, London, 1982, e.g. p. 277.
4 Translation as in S.Z. Ehler & J.B. Morrall, ed., *Church and State through the Centuries. A Collection of historic documents with commentaries*, London, 1954, p. 285. See E.E.Y. Hales, *Pio Nono*, London, 1954, especially pp. 255-62.
5 Odo Russell to Earl Russell, 13 Feb. 1865 in N. Blakiston, ed., *The Roman Question*, London, 1962, p. 307.

Professor Derek Beales. Sidney Sussex College, Cambridge.

Postscript ─────────

History: the *Useful* Subject

A GREAT MYTH about school subjects stalks the land. It runs: 'History is not a useful subject'. The assumption is that students choose History on grounds of interest and enjoyment, not because they expect (prospective teachers apart) to use it in later life. This has malign consequences at the next stage. At University Open Days history tutors are frequently confronted by concerned parents who ask, doubtfully, whether the subject their daughter or son wishes to read has any use. Parents' assumptions are only too clear.

Yet History's usefulness is clear. The problem is that it is too rarely articulated. Historians are too self-effacing - or possibly too arrogant - to be keen on 'selling' their subject. Yet it needs to be sold, not because universities need to fill their courses (they are full already), but so that students themselves should be aware both of practical skills they can expect to acquire and of the general value of History as a critical subject. Very many points could be made but, in the space available, only three will be briefly developed. These are offered in ascending order of practical importance.

1. *Acquaintance with a common culture:* Only people who have a reasonable acquaintance with the main landmarks of change in past societies can plug themselves into debate and discussion about the modern world. Without a 'map of the past' it is exceedingly difficult to understand issues of contemporary importance. How much better equipped to make sense of the bewildering kaleidoscope of frantic change in contemporary Russia is the person who knows something of previous attempts at change and reform from Peter the Great,

through Alexander II, Lenin, Stalin and the Communist experiment. Notice how many references in our serious newspapers actually *require* a historical perspective in order to be properly understood. Every aspect of our present has its past. Understanding what factors make for change and what for stability and how timeless personal characteristics such as self-interest and ambition have affected national destinies provide a powerful bond between the present and the past. We need to know in what ways the circumstances we face are unique and to what extent it is profitable to learn from similar experiences in the past. It may not be true that historians' skills equip us to predict the future. It certainly is true that systematic study of cause and consequence, similarity and difference are essential elements in making sense of the present. We are the inescapable product of our past and we cannot afford to ignore its lessons.

2. *The ability to explain logically and with cogency:* Students of history necessarily read a lot. Their training involves a great deal both of reading and writing. Virtually all positions of responsibility in industry and administration require fluency in the use of language. Reports must be written, positions defended and policy decisions explained. Historians are highly valued in these fields precisely because they make themselves skilled in presentation and argument and because they rarely see things in the oversimplified polarities of black and white. The ability to write skilfully and pointedly is not so prevalent among otherwise well-educated people as once it was, not least because many more vehicles of potent communication - visual and aural - now exist. Yet every organisation has need both of a written record and of well-presented material. Historians' acquaintance with the nuances of language, their abilities to infer potent messages from the 'tone' of a record and their skills of synthesis and analysis place them in a strong position when exposition and advocacy is required.

3. *The ability to come to well-supported judgements based on inadequate evidence:* At first sight, this may seem an abstruse skill. In reality, it is vital and here the Historian has a unique advantage. Historians' training require them to make judgements. Every essay should be the expression of sophisticated, and appropriately supported, opinion. Definitive conclusions are rarely possible and the intellectual flexibility which necessarily develops when one is concerned

with probability, or even possibility, rather than certainty, is a valuable asset. Consider the close parallels with the worlds of industry and commerce. Both operate competitively and many important decisions - how to develop a new product; whether to change the marketing strategy; how to evaluate factors which might support rationalisation, amalgamation or merger, for example - have necessarily to be taken without knowledge of the counter-strategies of competitors. Historians are specially expert in evaluating the factors necessary to reach a plausible judgement on the basis of deficient, incomplete or conflicting evidence. The past is necessarily reconstructed from an incomplete record. Those intuitive, judgmental skills which are at the basis of a persuasive case are directly transferable to the world of business. Though the parallels are not in every respect exact, many of the intellectual processes involved are identical.

The next time that you are asked 'What is the point of studying History?', therefore, I hope that you can present a powerful and effective response. By all means, study History because you *enjoy* it. Do not, however, indulge yourself by thinking that enjoyment need be its own reward. You are acquiring valuable skills which others need and are prepared to reward. You are *useful* as well as informed members of society. It is high time that historians stopped selling their subject short!

Professor Eric Evans. University of Lancaster.

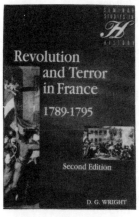

Discover where Bismarck went wrong in history . . .

• In *History Review*, a magazine for all History students at A Level and the undergraduate years.

• Distinguished historians bring clarity to debates and analyse the key issues of British and European History - from 1450 to the present.

• *History Review*, a valuable complement to texts and monographs for A Level teachers, students and undergraduates.

Illustrations, maps, charts and diagrams in black and white and colour illuminate the text.

History Review *keeps its subscribers up-to-date in the world of History and brings to life historical debates. Order today!*

Published in September, December and March.

Write for information, including current subscription rates, to:

History Review Subscriptions
20 Old Compton Street, London W1V 5PE